Therapist's Guide to Self-Care

Therapist's Guide to Self-Care

Lillie Weiss, Ph.D.

Cover photo: © Cindy Kassab/CORBIS
Cover design: Elise Weinger

Published in 2004 by
Brunner-Routledge
29 West 35th Street
New York, NY 10001
www.brunner-routledge.com

Published in Great Britain by
Brunner-Routledge
27 Church Road
Hove, East Sussex
BN3 2FA
www.brunner-routledge.co.uk

Brunner-Routledge is an imprint of the Taylor & Francis Group.
Printed in the United States of America on acid-free paper.

10 9 8 7 6 5 4 3 2 1

Library of Congress Cataloging-in-Publication Data

Weiss, Lillie.
Therapist's guide to self-care / Lillie Weiss.
p. cm.
Includes bibliographical references.
ISBN 0-415-94800-2 (Hardback)
1. Psychiatrists—Job stress—Prevention. 2. Psychiatrists—Mental health. I. Title.
RC451.4.P79W35 2004
616.89'0232—dc22

2003022170

For all the therapists
who have taught and mentored me
and whom I have taught and counseled

Contents

Acknowledgments

I want to thank all of the therapists who have contributed to this book. Their names are too numerous to mention, and confidentiality prohibits me from listing many by name. I am particularly grateful to all of you who have taken the time to respond to my questions and provide specific advice for beginning therapists. Your suggestions are sprinkled throughout the book. I also want to say thank you to Barry and Ez for your love, moral support, and technical assistance.

In addition, I thank everyone at Brunner-Routledge who has worked on my manuscript. I would like to thank Dr. George Zimmar for seeing the promise in it and for his astute and excellent recommendations to make it better. I also thank Dana Bliss for being so helpful in responding to all my questions and for his contributions to the project. I am grateful to Shannon Vargo for her hard work in refining and improving the manuscript, for her very helpful suggestions, and for her patience with the computer glitches. Special thanks goes to Patti Waldygo for her thorough and skillful editing of my manuscript and to both Erin Herlihy and Naomi Lynch for coordinating the project from manuscript to bound book. I am indebted to all of the staff at Brunner-Routledge, those I have worked with directly as well as those behind the scenes, for working so hard on my book and for bringing it to life.

Introduction

If we don't take care of ourselves, we can't take care of our clients.
—Karen Saakvitne, psychologist

Are you thinking of becoming a psychotherapist? Or are you in graduate school and wondering whether to continue? Maybe you are already working as a therapist and feel burned out. Perhaps you are in private practice or thinking of starting one. At various times I have been in all of these roles and have talked to people who have experienced these different situations. The purpose of this book is to offer you sound self-care strategies to ensure satisfaction in your work.

In my 30-plus years as a practicing psychologist, I have worked with mental health professionals in several different capacities: as a supervisor, a teacher, and a therapist. Currently, a large percentage of my practice consists of psychotherapists in various stages of their careers. The questions they raise range from nitty-gritty, practical ones, such as, "How do I set up my office procedures?" or "How do I deal with last-minute cancellations and no shows?" to deeper emotional concerns, such as, "How can I keep from getting emotionally drained and still remain empathetic?" "How do I handle all the conflicting demands and still make time for myself?" or "How do I cope with financial insecurities?"

Psychotherapy is becoming an increasingly stressful profession. Time pressures, excessive workload, and a sense of enormous responsibility are only part of the picture. The advent of managed care in recent years has only exacerbated the problem, resulting for many therapists in more paperwork and less income and control. Listening to emotionally demanding stories day in and day out brings added stress, often resulting in "vicarious traumatization" or "compassion fatigue," where clinicians vicariously experience the losses and traumas faced by their clients. Although the stresses are more pronounced for beginning therapists, even seasoned practitioners are vulnerable.

Psychologist Robert Epstein (1997) surveys the emotional toll that practicing therapy takes on people's lives and cites some troubling statistics about therapists' well-being:

- At least three out of four psychotherapists have experienced major distress within the last 3 years, and over 60% have suffered a clinically significant depression at some point.
- Mental health professionals commit suicide at an abnormally high rate, with psychiatrists killing themselves at rates about twice those expected of physicians.
- Psychologists are also at risk, with 1 out of 4 having suicidal feelings at times and 1 out of 16 attempting suicide.
- Female psychologists seem to be particularly vulnerable: The only published data show their rate of suicide to be three times that of the general population. This does not appear to be the case for male psychologists.

My experience with male and female practitioners is consistent with this trend. Although I have supervised and taught therapists of both genders, the overriding majority of mental health professionals who have come to me for therapy have been females (even though my hunch is that male therapists are prone to the same stresses as their female counterparts). It is for this reason that most of the examples in the text concern female clinicians.

In this book, I discuss therapist concerns and questions that keep cropping up and provide some practical tools that have worked for me and other mental health professionals. In addition to drawing on the research in this field and combining it with my own experiences, I have surveyed 15 experienced practitioners whom I respect about the stresses of being a therapist, what strategies have worked for them, and what advice they would give other therapists to help them become happier, more effective, and more successful in their work. This group included psychologists, psychiatrists, and social workers in both the public and the private sector. I also talked to many other practitioners without asking them to put their responses in writing. Some suggestions may seem to be more applicable to new therapists; however, even seasoned clinicians need reminders and will find these helpful.

First, a few words about my background: I have been a therapist for over 30 years. After receiving my Ph.D. in clinical psychology in 1968, I worked for 15 years at a number of inpatient and outpatient settings with a wide range of client populations before going into private practice. I was also simultaneously working at a university psychology department for some of those years, both before and after I went into private practice.

During almost all of my years as a psychologist, I have been actively engaged in the training and supervision of graduate students, psychology and counseling interns, psychiatry residents, and other psychotherapists, in my roles as faculty member of a medical center or a university psychology department, as well as in my own practice.

The book is divided into three parts. Part I helps you design and create the job you want and gives examples of therapists who have done that. Parts II and III provide you with tools and strategies to make those changes. Part II examines the stresses inherent in the psychotherapy profession and asks you to take stock of those operating in your life. The chapters in Part II provide you with tips on managing your outer environment: setting up your work and your life in such a way as to enhance your general well-being. These tips deal with creating an environment you love where you can express yourself, doing what you love and deleting the tasks that drain you, making your calendar your most important tool, and learning to set limits, among other topics. In Part III, I offer tools for managing your inner life to deal with some of the inevitable stresses of your work. These chapters provide you with practical advice, which includes, among other issues central to therapists, learning to recognize and avoid burnout, keeping a healthy distance, getting out of the overresponsibility trap, and coping with uncertainty.

These suggestions are not just for your benefit but for the well-being of your clients. As a therapist, you need to create a safe and comfortable environment for those who come to you for help, and you are a big part of that environment. If you are distracted, are fatigued, or have trouble listening to or remembering what your clients tell you because of your own burnout, your clients suffer. If you seem disinterested, overwhelmed, or unhappy, they may not wish to confide in you and burden you further with their problems. Clients notice your behavior and pick up subtle cues from you. As one woman told me, "I don't want to see a therapist whose plants are dying." You need to nurture yourself so that you can nurture your plants—and your clients!

It is important that clinicians take care of themselves not only for their sake but for the sake of their clients. When you are a happy therapist, everyone benefits. Whether you are entering the profession, are already in it, or are getting out gracefully—or know someone who is—it is my hope you will put to good use these strategies that have worked for me and others.

Part I

Designing and Creating the Life You Want

CHAPTER 1

Visualize the Life You Want and DO IT!

The first step to getting the things you want out of life is this: Decide what you want.

—Ben Stein

"I don't know if I can even say it out loud," said Lisa,* a psychologist who usually has no difficulty expressing her feelings. It took several sessions and lots of prodding before she could even verbalize the unthinkable: "I don't know if I want to be a psychologist any longer. I don't think I can do this the rest of my life." Lisa's reluctance to even *voice* the problem was understandable. After all, she had spent many, many years training to become a psychologist. The time, money, and energy she had invested toward her goal had been tremendous. No wonder she couldn't even allow herself to admit that she couldn't stand her job: It was her very *identity.*

Lisa might have been relieved to know that her feelings were not unique and are shared by many of her colleagues. In a large national survey of clinical psychologists, 4 out of 10 said they would choose a different career if they had their lives to live over (Norcross & Prochaska, 1982). Over the years, I have heard therapists express Lisa's concerns in one form or another, whether these are done in a joking manner or in earnest. "I think I'll close up shop and open a catering business," a therapist will say. Being a tour guide, making flower arrangements, working in a bookstore—fantasies of these and other less stressful jobs are common in casual conversation among clinicians.

In fact, some of my colleagues have done just that—left the mental health field entirely. However, short of taking such a drastic step, are there other alternatives to cope with the thoughts that occupy most clinicians from time to time—that they just want to escape and can't do this any longer?

---

*Names and details have been changed to protect identities.

If you are feeling like Lisa did or have at times felt "I just can't see myself doing this for the rest of my life," I would ask you, as I did Lisa, not to throw out the baby with the bath water and leave the mental health arena altogether—at least, not just yet—before exploring how many of the emotions you are experiencing are symptoms of burnout and how many have to do with the psychotherapy field itself.

I first asked Lisa to describe her work. Lisa had a fairly established practice and had contracts with several agencies to provide services for patients and their families. Because many of her clients were disabled, she often had to drive long distances to their settings to see them. She regularly got called on emergencies, and, in addition, she had the unpleasant task of informing relatives about the poor prognosis of their loved ones. Naturally, much of the families' anger and frustration was directed at her. Lisa felt an enormous amount of responsibility, even though she knew that she had no control over her clients' long-standing chronic conditions.

Lisa's work pervaded her home life as well, as she would frequently get phone calls and faxes at all hours of the day. In fact, there seemed to be no separation between her home and her work life. Because she was so busy during the week, she couldn't attend to her paperwork. She frequently ended up spending much of her weekend writing reports and letters and tending to other administrative details. Not surprisingly, this had started to cause problems in her marital relationship. Lisa had very little time for her husband or for herself and felt little control over what free moments she had because she thought that she had to be available and had to respond to any messages that came through. Most of the situations she got called on were quite depressing, and sometimes the intensity of the conditions would overwhelm her.

Lisa did not allow herself to say no to referrals; after all, she was in private practice and had to make a living. What if she didn't get any more clients? She had no steady paycheck and got anxious if there were any empty spaces in her schedule. Lisa was feeling increasingly burned out and frustrated; there seemed to be so many demands on her time and energy. She hated the emotions that she, a very empathetic and caring person, was beginning to develop toward her clients. Everyone seemed to want something from her, including her husband. She saw his wanting her time and attention as "one more demand." Unfortunately, he was the one person she most often said no to. She also had no energy for her friends and started feeling increasingly isolated.

Lisa's work situation had all the elements necessary to produce full-blown burnout: time pressures, lack of control over her work schedule, a tremendous sense of responsibility, financial insecurities, and social isolation, with few apparent rewards (Maslach & Leiter, 1997). Lisa, who had always loved psychology, was beginning to dread going to work. In fact, she was beginning to dread her life.

"If you could design your life any way you could, how would you do it?" I asked her. "If time and money were no object, how would you create the life you want?" Until this point, Lisa had no idea that she could in fact fashion her existence and make it exactly the way she wanted. She was, after all, her own boss, and it was entirely up to her to decide her hours, her schedule, the types of clients she saw, and how she chose to fill up her days. What aspects of her current job would she keep? What would she throw out? What nonwork activities would she make time for?

Lisa said that if she could design her life any way she wanted, she would exercise and do meditation every morning before she set out for work, and she would come home from work earlier and have her evenings and weekends free to do whatever she wanted. In addition, she would structure her work so that she would see clients 2 days a week, do paperwork and reports the other 2 days, and take 1 day off for herself to pursue other interests, such as computer classes. She would eliminate all of the cases that involved a lot of driving to appointments (and consequently were not cost-effective, generating very little income), as well as those she found emotionally draining.

"DO IT!" Lisa almost immediately implemented those changes once she recognized that she was, in fact, in charge of her life and could tailor it any way she wanted. She scheduled patients only on Mondays and Wednesdays and left Tuesdays and Thursdays for reports, phone calls, and other administrative chores. Because she had control over when to start her day, she began every morning with exercise and meditation before heading off for work, and when she came home, she turned off the faxes and the computer, leaving the paperwork for Tuesdays and Thursdays. She signed up for a computer class on her free day. She also informed her referral sources that she was only driving to settings close to her home and, in addition, outlined what types of cases she would see in the future. When she got "emergency" calls, she scheduled to see those patients on Mondays or Wednesdays, instead of disrupting her day completely and attending to the emergencies immediately.

Besides making changes in her outer environment, Lisa also made some inner changes in her behavior and attitudes. She said no to new referrals that she found to be too emotionally draining. She also learned to cope with her feelings of financial insecurity, recognizing that if she filled up her schedule with cases that drained her, there would be no room for those that exhilarated her. To her relief, she suffered no financial setbacks and managed to fill up her schedule with activities she liked. She also learned to cope with her feelings of overresponsibility for her patients by telling herself, "I didn't make them disabled, and I cannot fix their situation." Consequently, she was able to deal with the anger expressed by their relatives and not take it so personally. Within a few weeks, Lisa was feeling enthusiastic about her work and her life again. "I feel excited about what I'm doing," she said, a far cry from the dread she described when she first came to see me. Not only did she feel good about her job, but her relationship with her spouse improved as well because she was able to give more to her marriage.

Lisa's story comes in many different shapes and forms. Although Lisa's level of burnout was quite pronounced, you may have felt like her at different times in your career. It is a rare therapist who has not experienced some of those emotions to some degree at some point or another. Whether you feel as stressed as Lisa was or only minimally burned out, or you merely want to make an already satisfying career even better, the first step is to visualize the kind of life you want. The next step is to DO IT! In the following chapters, I will provide tools to help you make those changes.

When you can see in your mind's eye exactly how you would like your life to be, then you can make it a reality. Visualization is one of the most powerful tools for putting your ideas into action. Research has shown that people have used it successfully to help them realize their goals, whether those are to improve a golf score, overcome a phobia, lose weight, or even shrink malignant tumors (Samuels & Samuels, 1992). When you can see yourself doing what you love, it serves as a mental practice or a rehearsal for you, because you have already done it in your mind. That makes it easier for you to do the "real" thing.

The next two chapters are brief and consist mainly of self-assessments to help you visualize and fine-tune this process of making your dream a reality. At the end of every chapter in the book, there will be questions you can ask yourself to help you summarize the suggestions and apply them to your own life.

CHAPTER 2

Ask Yourself: "If Money Were No Object . . ."

It's only money.

—Jackie Bradley, retired social worker

If you were guaranteed a steady, comfortable income for life, how would you structure your days? Would you still work? How many hours a week would you work? How would you fill up your time? What activities would you include in your schedule?

What would you make more time for? What would you eliminate? Would you remain in your profession or change careers? What kind of environment would you work in? Close your eyes for a few minutes and think about what would be an ideal situation for you. For the moment, don't let reality and financial concerns get in the way. Just allow your mind to wander and think of how you would like your dream job to be.

I have often been surprised by how close people's ideal job is to what they are already doing. Most therapists to whom I've put the question usually respond, as Lisa did, that they would put in less hours, start later or end earlier, not work with certain populations, make time for other interesting activities, or any number of changes that would be fairly easy to implement if they gave themselves permission to do so.

Irene is a case in point. Irene loved her work very much. She had recently set up a private practice in her home and enjoyed the variety and the stimulation it offered her. She took good care of herself and seldom felt burned out. On the contrary, her work exhilarated her. However, her career came at some personal sacrifice. Irene and her husband owned a small vacation home several thousand miles away, where she used to spend her summers before she went into private practice. It was a quiet hideaway in the woods where she went to recharge her batteries and which was very important to her emotional and spiritual well-being. Irene didn't feel that she could leave every summer now that she had a full-time practice. "Why not?" I asked her. "I don't know," she said. "I just assumed it wasn't possible." Like Lisa, Irene had set her own roadblocks to fulfilling her fantasies and creating her dream job. What, in fact, was keeping Irene from leaving every summer? In her case, it wasn't the income, because she lived very frugally. She also didn't have any clients who would not be able to manage without a few weeks of therapy. Instead of worrying about why she *couldn't* make her dream come true, Irene now focused on how she *could,* which, surprisingly, just as in Lisa's case, only involved some planning and taking action. Irene developed a strategy to implement her plan of going away in the summer. She prepared all of her clients in advance and told them that she would be gone during the months of July and August. She made arrangements for another therapist to cover for her if needed, and she also arranged telephone appointments with a few of her clients. In addition, she told all prospective referrals that she would be gone over the summer, leaving it up to them whether they wished to see her or find a different therapist. To her delight, most of them opted to come to her. Instead of focusing on why she couldn't have a dream job, Irene spent her energies planning how to make her dream come true.

Lisa and Irene are like many other therapists: bright, competent, resourceful, and insightful. Once they figured out what they needed to do, they immediately set out to do it. Many of the changes simply involved making schedule adjustments and informing others about them. Lisa and Irene were both in private practice—they were their own bosses—and they didn't need anybody else's permission to do what they wanted. In both cases, there was little or no monetary fallout from making the minor adjustments to their jobs—in Lisa's case because she spent less time driving, and in Irene's situation because she lived frugally and had saved for this block of time. However, the emotional payoffs of these changes were tremendous.

Whereas not every therapist who wants to create the ideal job has as much freedom to do so as Lisa and Irene did, even psychotherapists with less financial flexibility can modify their job to make it closer to the one of their dreams.

Sheila was a financially strapped single mother who needed to work to support herself and her two sons. She was a very talented and creative individual, and her full-time job in an agency with crisis patients depleted her energies and didn't make full use of her abilities. Sheila would have liked to work fewer hours so that she could spend more time with her children. Her dream job would have been to have her own practice, where she would see a few clients every week and spend the rest of her time teaching, conducting workshops, or doing research. She had an analytical mind and enjoyed the stimulation that academic work provided. Sheila's plan took longer to implement than Lisa's or Irene's did. First of all, she started looking for another job with less burnout conditions and more flexible hours. She found a position working 4 days a week, and although it wasn't exactly what she wanted, it paid well and also had better hours; she could come home earlier and spend time with her children. On her free day, Sheila actively pursued her other goals. She made a few contacts, soon landing some teaching assignments that she enjoyed very much and felt made full use of her talents. As she developed more teaching contacts, she was able to gradually cut back on her job. Although Sheila's current work situation is still not "perfect"—she would prefer to work fewer hours—it is a far cry from her previous position, and she is much happier.

Ask yourself, "If money were no object, how would I design my life?" Then make a plan and DO IT! Whether self-limiting beliefs like Lisa's and Irene's, or reality and monetary concerns like Sheila's, are keeping you from creating your dream job, make a plan and follow it. Deliberate on the best way to make your vision a reality.

Self-Assessment

Take a few minutes to visualize the ideal life for you. What would you do if you didn't have to worry about making a living?

If money were no object, how would I design my life?

Would I still work? If yes, how many hours a week would I work?

What activities would I include in my schedule?

What activities would I eliminate?

Would I remain in my profession or change careers?

What kind of an environment would I work in?

What would I like to do with my leisure time?

What outer obstacles (e.g., time or money) are keeping me from making my dream job a reality?

What inner obstacles (e.g., fears, self-limiting beliefs) are keeping me from living the life I want?

What can I do to deal with these inner concerns?

CHAPTER 3

Hire Yourself as Your Life Manager

A man is a success if he gets up in the morning and goes to bed at night and in between does what he wants to do.

—Bob Dylan

To help you implement your plan to make your dream job a reality, pretend that you are your own client. What advice would you give yourself? What adjustments would you like to make? What plan would you devise to put those changes into action? Phillip McGraw, in his book *Life Strategies* (1999), suggests looking at yourself as if you were two different people and managing your life as if you were your own client. Thinking of yourself as a "life manager" can give you the perspective to assess how you are doing.

Seeing yourself as a manager or a life consultant helps you take the necessary steps to structure and design your life to make it exactly the way you want. Like other psychotherapists, you counsel your clients every day on how to manage their worlds, and, probably more than a member of any other professional group, you have the skills and the expertise to form a plan to make life changes.

Self-Assessment

Ask yourself questions such as these, to appraise how well your manager is handling your life:

If I had to give my manager a performance evaluation, how would I rate him or her?

Is my manager taking care of my physical and emotional health?

Is my manager providing job opportunities for me that utilize my talents and help me grow professionally?

Is my manager creating a work environment that I enjoy and that is conducive to my mental health?

Is my manager designing my schedule so that I have time for the things I enjoy?

Is my manager structuring my life so that there is balance in it?

Is my manager arranging for me to have fun?

Is my manager organizing my life in a way that enables me to perform at my best, allowing me to be an effective therapist, spouse, parent, or friend?

Take a few minutes to make a plan to create the dream job you want for your most important client, yourself. Write it down. Be as specific as possible. Put down what steps you need to take to make those things happen. What *exactly* do you need to do, for example, if you want to take an afternoon off every week? Is it as simple as not scheduling clients that afternoon? Do you need to talk to your boss, if you have one? If your goal is to write or teach a few hours every week, what steps do you need to take to make that happen? Make a plan and DO IT!

What is my plan to create my dream job?

What concrete steps do I need to take to make that happen?

In the following chapters, I will provide you with tips and strategies that have worked for me and other therapists to help make your plan a reality. Part II has suggestions for managing your external environment, and Part III focuses on managing your inner world to create the life and the job you want.

Part II

Tips for Managing Your Outer Environment

CHAPTER 4

Do the Things You Enjoy and Eliminate Those That Drain You

Life is too short for bad wine.

—Anonymous

This chapter lists the rewards and the hassles inherent in being a therapist, asks you to take stock of these in your own life, and helps you to take action to increase the joys and decrease the negatives. Every profession has its problems and its satisfactions, and the mental health field is no exception. Psychologists Kramen-Kahn and Hansen (1998) list the main categories of stresses and rewards, as well as the most frequently endorsed ones among psychotherapists. Their advice? Minimize hazards, maximize rewards.

Before exploring their lists further, I would like to highlight the following point so that you do not get a lopsided view, especially because I devote more pages in this chapter to describing the hassles than I do to the satisfactions. Although the authors list both pluses and minuses, *it is significant that the rewards were endorsed by 39% to 93% of respondents, whereas the hazards were endorsed by 19% to 29%. This certainly suggests that in spite of the long list of stresses, psychotherapy is an intrinsically satisfying field.*

Let us take a look at the authors' list of the different stress categories for psychotherapists. Therapist occupational stresses tend to fall into five main areas: business-related problems, client-related issues, the personal challenges of the psychotherapist (e.g., constant giving), setting-related stresses (e.g., excessive workload), and evaluation-related problems (e.g., difficulty assessing client progress). These pressures take their toll on both therapists and their clients (Farber, 1990; Guy, Poelstra, & Stark, 1989; Kottler, 1993; Mahoney, 1997; Sherman, 1996; Sussman, 1993). In one study (Pope, Tabachnik, & Keith-Spiegel, 1987), a large percentage of psychologists—60%—said they have worked when they were too distressed to be effective, thereby shortchanging their clients.

In Kramen-Kahn and Hansen's (1998) survey of 208 clinicians, the most frequently endorsed occupational hazards seemed to be in the business- and setting-related categories, as follows: business aspects, economic insecurity, professional conflicts, time pressures, a sense of enormous responsibility, excessive workload, and case uncertainties. These are only part of the picture, the tip of the iceberg. Whereas these may be the most *frequently* endorsed stresses, they are not necessarily the ones that take the most emotional toll on therapists. Client-related issues, such as having a homicidal or a suicidal patient, though occurring less frequently, may have more of an impact.

In my conversations with and informal surveys of other therapists, many mentioned fairly serious concerns, some of which had to do with their own physical vulnerability, as well as that of their clients. Most practitioners listed suicidal clients, fear for their own and their patients' safety, or both, as the most significant hazards of their profession.

Sam, a psychologist whose patient killed himself, could not even bring himself to talk about it with his colleagues until months later. "To say that I was devastated is an understatement. I kept going over and over in my mind what had happened and was there something I missed and what I could have done to prevent it. I know it wasn't my fault, and that if he was intent on doing it, there was nothing I could do about it. But I still felt guilty," he said. "I felt I had failed somehow, and I was also afraid of how others would judge me. And, of course, there was the fear—rational or not—that I would get sued, that I was responsible for what he did." Sam's fears were not entirely unfounded. His feelings of sadness and guilt were compounded by shame and fear of reprisal.

Dealing with difficult clients is at the top of the list of stressors for most of the therapists I surveyed, whether these constitute patients who threaten suicide or those with such entrenched destructive personality patterns that they evoke an ongoing feeling of dread in your interactions with them. Working with volatile patients or ones with excessive dependency needs can deplete even the most patient and emotionally grounded clinician. So can seeing a large number of clients who have been victimized by abuse or those with terminal illnesses.

Clients who threaten your safety can be extremely stressful, and some of the therapists I surveyed listed being stalked and threatened by their patients as a major stressor. Unfortunately, this problem is not all that uncommon. Half of all therapists have at some point received threats of physical violence from their clients, and roughly 40% are actually attacked (Guy, Brown, & Poelstra, 1990, 1992). More recent studies show an even higher incidence of violent acts and are consistent with previous research findings that predict that *6 out of 10 mental health providers will be assaulted during their professional careers* (Arthur, Brende, & Quiroz, 2003).

A number of practitioners have been victimized by harrassment from the people they treat, ranging from being the object of their clients' "obsessional following" (Meloy & Gothard, 1995) to more serious threats of physical injury. Stalking of mental health professionals by their clients, although relatively infrequent—studies on the prevalence range from 5.6 to 13% (Corder & Whiteside, 1996; Lion & Hirschler, 1998; Romans, Hayes, & White, 1996)—can have serious psychological consequences, not to mention physical ones, if the threats are carried out (Gentile, Asamen, Harmell, & Weathers, 2002). Even if only 1 in 10 or 20 clinicians is stalked, that is still a very large number! Any therapist can be the unwitting target of a patient's delusions or rage, and the nightmare of being stalked or physically attacked can have severe repercussions.

John and Lena are two therapists whose lives changed dramatically following such incidents. John was interviewing a hospitalized patient when the man reached for his throat and attempted to strangle him. Fortunately for John, a nurse walked by and saved his life. The assault took its toll on his emotional and physical health, and John suffered a heart attack shortly afterward. Following months of post-traumatic stress, John decided to retire. Lena was harrassed and stalked by one of her patients for months. He followed her everywhere, and her calling the police and putting out a restraining order on him did not deter his movements. Lena changed telephone numbers, offices, residences—all to no avail. He always managed to trace her down. She eventually left the state and the profession entirely. Rumors have it that she changed her name and went into hiding. These are, of course, fairly extreme examples. However, they did and do happen.

Not only are mental health professionals attacked verbally and physically, in today's current climate, the threat of litigation is ever present (Otto & Schmidt, 1991; Soisson, VandeCreek, & Knapp, 1987). So is the fear of having a complaint filed against you. False but credible claims of misconduct against therapists are not only possible but are frequently used by purported victims for their personal agendas (Williams, 2000). Whereas 20 or 30 years ago, these fears were virtually nonexistent, they are in the back of many therapists' minds today in this increasingly suit-happy society. Next to suicidal or homicidal clients, the litigious aspects of the profession were frequently mentioned as significant stressors by therapists. Comments such as these were common in response to my questions to clinicians on what they considered to be some of the most significant stresses or hassles of being a therapist:

"It's very hard to be a psychologist today—the litigious aspects scare me."

". . . when angry patients begin to describe the tremendous disappointment they have over past professional treatment, along with complaints they have made to lawyers and other professional groups."

". . . having a patient whom I have treated for many years through a lifetime of crises, saving his marriage, treating other members of his family—commit suicide—and having his children threatening to sue me for his death!"

"I always do everything with the threat of malpractice litigation in the back of my mind."

Lorraine had been treating a woman in therapy who was going through an unhappy marriage. When the marriage broke up, the woman's husband, an attorney, filed a lawsuit, blaming Lorraine for the demise of the union. Although he probably didn't have a legal leg to stand on, this did not prevent him from making Lorraine's life miserable for months on end. She was constantly hounded by phone calls, subpoenas, and requests for information, as well as implicit threats, and had to hire an attorney herself. The cost in time, money, paperwork, and general aggravation was profound.

Although the business aspects of a practice and a sense of economic insecurity may not seem as traumatic as fears of personal or client safety or of being sued, they can nevertheless cause significant distress at times for therapists in private practice (Kramen-Kahn & Hansen, 1998; Nash, Norcross, & Prochaska, 1984), as evidenced by these comments about significant stressors:

"The ebb and flow of practice—the absence of consistency—some weeks too full others too empty."

"Dealing with patients about their insurance, which they usually expect to pay, and then do not. Why am I even in the loop?"

"Allowing some clients to accumulate a debt-balance, which potentially impacted treatment and occasionally went unpaid."

"Managed care–intrusion into case management and paperwork hassles."

"With no secretary—returning pages, phone calls and seeing patients with no breaks between sessions."

"No shows and last-minute cancellations."

"I can't stand the insurance hassles."

"Unpaid bills."

These comments just hint at the economic vulnerability that has only increased in recent years with the advent of managed care. A well-executed series of focus groups conducted across the United States under the auspices of the American Psychological Association (APA Practice Directorate & the Widmeyer Group, 1994) confirms what clinicians feel about the cost-cutting, workload-increasing pressures from managed care, of which financial insecurity is only one of the down sides.

Although therapists working in an agency may not have the same financial or business stresses experienced by their peers who work for themselves, they have other hassles, including increased workload, bureaucratic mazes, conflicts with coworkers, and, frequently, a lack of control, which is a major component in stress and burnout (Maslach & Leiter, 1997). A national survey of psychotherapists found that those working in institutional clinical settings are less satisfied with psychotherapy as a career than are their counterparts in independent practice (Norcross & Prochaska, 1983). It is noteworthy that when I asked clinicians who worked in non–private practice environments what was most stressful for them, they immediately replied, "The setting," "the system," or "the organization." Here is a sample of their comments:

"I have no stress from my patients. It's my coworkers who drive me nuts."

"The system . . . the excessive workload, the paperwork . . ."

"The bureaucracy . . . the frustrations of working in a system."

"Being in a system—my coworkers and the regulations of the system are more stressful than the clients."

These remarks are not surprising. Therapists working in some systems often do not have the same amount of control over their work conditions that those in private practice do, and it is well-known that uncontrollable stressors are more damaging than those under our influence (Seligman, 1975). In addition, a large workload or interpersonal conflict on the job can result in anxiety, physical problems, and dissatisfaction with the job (Spector, Dwyer, & Jex, 1988). So can organizational constraints, those job conditions that may make it difficult or impossible to do your job (O'Connor, Peters, Rudolf, & Pooyan, 1982), be they a difficult boss, insufficient staff or equipment, conflicting demands, or a myriad of stressors outside your control. Frequently, negative workplace communication can result in increased burnout or a decision to leave (Geurts, Schaufeli, & De Jonge, 1998).

Although individuals working for themselves do not have to deal with "systems" (other than managed-care or insurance companies, if they choose to), private practice has its own special burnout problems that do not occur as much for persons working in organizations: a sense of isolation and a lack of diversity in activities (Guy, 1987; Kottler, 1993; Yalom, 2002). Agencies often provide their own social support through other colleagues and frequently have a built-in variety of tasks: conferences, meetings, teaching, research, and other things to do besides listening to clients hour after hour. Research shows that it is not the number of hours you work but the number of hours seeing clients that contributes to burnout (Maslach, 1976). Therapists in private practice do not usually have the full range of activities available to those employed in other organizations.

Whether you are working for an agency or are self-employed, just being a therapist can cause significant stresses (Guy, Freudenberger, Farber, & Norcross, 1990), as seen by some of these comments:

"I feel inadequate to the task."

"I can't stand to listen to one more story."

"I sometimes feel there is nothing left to give."

"How do I deal with this?"

Burnout, feelings of inadequacy, being overwhelmed . . . these and many more are the personal challenges of the psychotherapist, some more so at different times in our careers.

The stresses are especially pronounced for newcomers to the field. Not only do they have to deal with the general anxiety of mastering skills, they may also be inundated with the realities of running a practice (Kottler & Hazler, 1997), as well as, in some instances, very demanding licensure and board-certification requirements, particularly for psychologists. In a study comparing earnings and the amount of time to complete requirements across 13 professions, it was found that psychologists have an unusually long period of preparation, coupled with incomes that do not measure up to their training, with the authors questioning whether we have raised the bar too far (De Vaney Olvey, Hogg, & Counts, 2002). Certainly, the studies on therapist stress consistently indicate more stress among new practitioners (Ackerley, Burnell, Holder, & Kurdek, 1988; Rodolfa, Kraft, & Reilley, 1988).

The news is not all bad. There are many factors—most of them intrinsic—that help clinicians enjoy their work. Occupational rewards tend to fall into six categories: feelings of effectiveness, ongoing self-development, professional autonomy-independence, opportunities for emotional intimacy, professional-financial recognition, and flexible, diverse work (Kramen-Kahn & Hansen, 1998).

Almost every therapist I talked to listed seeing clients improve as the main satisfaction of being a therapist, with comments such as these being common in listing the rewards of the profession:

> "Seeing patients grow and have productive lives."
>
> "Knowing you've made a difference in someone's life."
>
> "The privilege of participating in client change and successes."
>
> "Seeing people change."
>
> "Being in a life-changing profession."
>
> "Seeing clients do better in their marriages and in parenting."
>
> "Observing that therapy works. Knowing that what may seem hopeless can change with patience, perseverance, and use of self-knowledge, insight, and humanity."

The rewards of being a therapist seem to be inherent in the job itself (Radeke & Mahoney, 2000). In fact, many practitioners went so far as to say that if you do not enjoy the work, you should get out of the field. The main satisfaction in being a therapist is intrinsic. As one clinician who has been seeing patients for 40 years put it, "You should have an honest, deep regard for the individuals deep inside. You should really enjoy seeing them. If you don't, get out of the profession."

Promoting growth in clients was the most frequently endorsed item in Kramen-Kahn and Hansen's (1998) survey of rewards, listed by 93% of therapists, followed by enjoyment of the work (79%). Other frequently endorsed satisfactions ranked as follows: opportunity to continue to learn, challenging work, professional autonomy-independence, flexible hours, increased self-knowledge, variety in work and cases, personal growth, a sense of emotional intimacy, and being a role model and a mentor. To repeat what I said at the beginning of this chapter, *It is very significant that the rewards were endorsed by 39% to 93% of respondents, whereas the hazards were endorsed by 19% to 29%. Certainly, this suggests that in spite of the stresses, psychotherapy is an intrinsically satisfying field.*

Being connected to patients and learning from them is often as satisfying as seeing them improve, as can be seen from some of the responses to my questions as to the rewards of the profession:

"Learning from patients—a lot—and frequently."

"Feeling trusted, respected in a mutually satisfying and productive relationship."

"Having clients feel safe and comfortable working with me or challenging life issues."

"The feeling of being connected to another person as he or she shares something authentic and meaningful."

"My own personal growth, in my clients' educating me."

"The relationships with patients that develop. Their sharing shame, the intimacy."

The comments suggest that the act of doing therapy has its own rewards. As one therapist put it, "Contact with people is, for me, tremendously energizing and an antidepressant. I'm never burned out."

Besides the intrinsic rewards, there are also some external perks: colleagues, flexible hours, as well as variety in work. In fact, the mental health field can be tremendously diverse, not only in the type of client populations you see but in the number of activities available in addition to psychotherapy, such as assessment, teaching, supervising, research, writing, developing programs, and administration. Some of the new jobs for psychologists include consulting for cancer risk organizations, developing programs for military corporations, helping with jury selection, creating products on the Internet, and other innovative work, limited only by one's imagination.

Self-Assessment

As you looked at some of the hazards and the rewards of being a therapist, you may have identified with some of them in your particular situation. Take a look at your own stresses and satisfactions. Make a list of everything that is a hassle for you, big or small—whether it is something as simple as not having time between patients to return phone calls or as stressful as having a suicidal or volatile client. You might wish to mentally observe and monitor yourself over the next few days and note when you get that knot in your stomach or any other indication that you feel stressed. What gives you the most hassles? Is it worry over a client? Is it talking on the phone with an insurance clerk? Is it concern over finances? Is it feeling tired? Is it doing paperwork that seems meaningless? Is it your boss or coworker? Write down *anything and everything* that stresses you.

What are the hassles of my work?

Now make a list of all the rewards of being a therapist. When are the moments that you feel most energized? What do you enjoy most about your day? Is it talking to a colleague? Is it seeing a client improve? Is it a Christmas card you got from someone you saw in therapy years ago? Is it being absorbed in someone's story and feeling that you have made a difference? Is it the lunch you had with a coworker?

What are the rewards?

Now look at your two lists and make a plan to minimize the things that drain you and to increase the things that you enjoy doing! Deliberate on how you can make those changes. Some things you can do very quickly; others may take some planning or may be done in small steps. Be ruthless when you scrutinize your list, and eliminate all the hassles that are within your control. Make it your aim to be "toleration-free," as someone once put it—that is, to get rid of all the things you tolerate and settle for. Conversely, figure out how to maximize the rewards. If you enjoy learning, for example, how can you add more educational opportunities to your life? If colleagues energize you, how can you make more room for them? Remember, as you take out what you don't like, you are also making room for the things you love.

What hassles can I get rid of or minimize?

What is my action plan to decrease the hassles?

Which rewards can I increase?

What is my action plan to put more of what I enjoy into my life?

Some of the changes you make may require only minor modifications, such as taking more breaks, resigning from certain managed-care panels, screening certain clients, starting your day later, or any number of modifications that are fairly simple to implement. Other stresses may not be as easy to eliminate. If you are working in a toxic environment, one that undermines your emotional, spiritual, and physical well-being, you need to get out as soon as possible before it poisons you completely. Having both worked at and known others who have worked in these places, I understand how debilitating the effects of these sanity drainers can be. In these settings, you cannot just make a few modifications here and there. You need to eliminate the whole environment completely, by leaving it. Until you do, you will need to use some of the strategies mentioned in Part III—managing your inner environment—to help you maintain your equilibrium in the meantime.

If you are fortunate to be working in a setting you like or that you have control over, reducing the hazards and maximizing the satisfactions will make a big difference in your well-being and that of your clients. In the next few chapters, I will discuss further how to make the changes you want.

CHAPTER 5

Create an Environment You Love in Which You Can Express Yourself

Work is a natural vehicle for self-expression because we spend so much of our time in its thrall. It simply makes no sense to turn off our personality, squelch our real abilities, forget our need for stimulation and personal growth forty hours out of every week.

—Marsha Sinetar, *Do What You Love, the Money Will Follow*

Nearly 30 years ago, I was working 20 hours a week in a clinical position and the other 20 at a university job. One day, when I came to work, I discovered that the office where I saw clients had been changed. I had been moved to a room with a small screen dividing me from another employee, an accountant for the hospital I worked for. The "system," in its infinite wisdom, wanted to maximize office space and make working more efficient. The powers above decided that because I was a half-time employee, I needed only half an office. The fact that I had no privacy to do therapy seemed irrelevant. Needless to say, I left within a very short time because this was clearly an environment where I could not do my job. If one of the requirements of psychotherapy is having a safe place where clients can express themselves, this was one where neither the therapist nor the client could talk—literally—for fear of being heard.

This, of course, is an extreme example of surroundings that are not conducive to doing therapy. Other settings may not be "safe" in subtler ways. In the previous chapter, I discussed toxic systems—environments where you are unable to be yourself and where clients are ultimately affected. Whether the barrier is a thin partition or an intrusive managed-care network that makes it almost impossible for you or your clients to grow, you owe it to yourself and to them to either change the environment or leave it. There is strong support that the cause of burnout is often in the system, not in the individual, and the recommended course is to change organizations (Maslach & Leiter, 1997). Unfortunately, making organizational changes a practice has been one of the least-utilized strategies by clinicians (Brady, Norcross, & Guy, 1995).

It is very important for you to create an atmosphere where you can function at your best and, consequently, give the best to those you counsel. A few years ago, several therapists independently came to me for advice because they felt they could not be themselves in the setting they were working in. "I hate to admit this," they'd say, "but I'm embarrassed to be associated with that place. No matter how much I try to isolate myself from it, it still affects me—and I know it affects the patients as well." All of these therapists left and created their own environments—ones they loved, that reflected them, and where they and their clients were happy.

When I discuss an environment, I am not merely talking about the physical surroundings but about the psychological and spiritual atmosphere as well. Is this a place that has your best interests at heart? Is this a place that is nurturing? Does it provide you with enough stimulation to grow? Do you feel respected? Can you do your best work there? If you are working in a setting that is demeaning to you or your clients, what changes can you make? If that is not possible, leave!

Ask yourself what you can do to create a physical and emotional environment that will help you and your clients thrive. In Chapter 3, I discussed hiring yourself as your own manager. What can your manager do to make your surroundings as conducive to growth as possible? When you ask yourself this question, try your best to figure out which conditions are optimal for you. Are you a morning or an evening person? What distractions keep you from being at your best and thereby not attending fully to your clients? What kind of a climate do you need to maximize how well you work?

The importance of the physical environment on your health and your work cannot be overestimated, and researchers are using their knowledge in this area to design and plan settings better suited for human needs (Garling & Evans, 1991). Rachel and Stephen Kaplan have spent many years studying restorative environments and their effects on your physical and emotional well-being. Among other things, they found that just bringing nature into the office can rejuvenate you. Office workers with a view of nature liked their jobs more, were healthier, and felt more satisfied with their lives (Kaplan & Kaplan, 1989).

Judith Heerwagen, a psychologist, also utlizes the principles of restorative surroundings in the work she does as a consultant to designers and to companies. Not surprisingly, she finds that "naturalizing" buildings contributes to organizational success and productivity (Heerwagen, 2000). Other studies have found that "green" environments even help inner-city children delay gratification and inhibit impulses (Kuo &

Sullivan, 2001) and allow patients to heal faster after surgery (Ulrich, 1984, 1991). In short, a good physical environment is conducive to your mental and even physical health at times!

Create an environment that you love and that fully reflects you. Irene, for example, had an office that represented her and that she was most comfortable in. It was full of old, "funky" furniture, throw rugs, and large floor pillows, and it was essentially an extension of her personality. Clients either resonated to it—or didn't. But it was a place where she could truly be herself. It didn't fit the mold—but then, neither did she!

Joann, a therapist in private practice, also modified her environment to reflect the way she worked. "I can never finish on the hour," she said. "How do you do it?" I suggested getting several clocks and putting them on different sides of the room so that she could see the time from wherever she was sitting—something that usually works for me. She went out and bought herself some clocks but still had difficulty ending on time. Finally, she had an epiphany: "The way I work, it takes an hour till we really get warmed up and get to the meat of the matter." Joann did some very intensive work, and her sessions frequently demanded an hour and a half. "I started scheduling clients for 90 minutes instead of an hour. It works for me, and I don't feel rushed." Rather than trying to fit into a mold, Joann adapted the environment to her needs.

These examples are only variations on how therapists can create a physical setting that they love and that reflects them. For many clinicians, the office is a second home. Indeed, some therapists spend more time there than they do in their own house. Your work, like your home, is a reflection and an extension of your personality, and you need to be able to fully express yourself in both. Give as much care to creating a comfortable work environment as you do to your living environment. Strive to make your workplace as much a sanctuary as your home is.

No less important than your physical surroundings is the psychological environment. Experts on the workplace and the mental health of practitioners constantly emphasize the role of your work setting in your overall well-being. James Quick, a psychologist who specializes in workplace stress, finds that employees need to be healthy individuals in order to do a good job. To that end, they need to work in places where they can have positive relationships with others (Quick, Quick, & Hurrell, 1997). Guy (2000), an expert on the professional lives of psychotherapists, echoes the importance of a nurturing interpersonal environment in his self-care suggestions to them. As he states, "With a comprehensive self-care program for psychologists, it is best to deliberately maintain healthy ways to satisfy our longing for respect and nurturance within a network of vibrant relationships with loved ones and friends. This will enable us to 'hold the holding environment together' to the benefit of our clients and ourselves" (p. 352). Make certain that your work setting includes positive interactions with others!

If, as Freud said, love and work are our two basic needs, then your workplace should be as nurturant as your relationships. Where and how you do your job can be an expression of the many different aspects of your personality, your talents, and your beliefs; yet you may be allowing certain factors to get in the way of performing your tasks the way you would like to.

One intrusion into the way many therapists work is managed care. When managed care became the norm, I joined the bandwagon, as did many of my colleagues. Rather than doing therapy in my usual manner, which would be asking questions that I felt were most relevant to the therapy process, I instead had to focus on getting information that was important for the insurance companies. A basic given of therapy is that the client's needs should always come first. Clearly, gathering data for the managed-care companies, whether these were pertinent to the therapy issue or not, superseded the client's needs to talk. Being accountable to insurance companies meant I could not be myself and allow my clients to express themselves the way they wanted. Obviously, I could not participate in managed care and at the same time put the patient's needs first. I chose to get out of those toxic systems; otherwise, I would be shortchanging myself and my clients.

It is not enough just to leave toxic systems. You need to create an environment that will allow you to grow professionally. One of the conclusions emerging from years of research on practitioners is the importance of an open, supportive work environment for optimal professional development, one that allows you the time and the freedom to reflect on your experiences (Skovholt & Ronnestad, 2001). Are you in a setting where you have interactions with colleagues? If not, how can you do that? Are you learning new things all the time? If that's not the case, how can you arrange to have these types of experiences? Are you making full use of your skills and talents in your work? How can you maximize opportunities for you to do so?

Self-Assessment

Take a few minutes and ask yourself how you can create an environment that you love coming to and where you can express yourself and use your talents fully. Be as specific and as concrete as possible. Under what conditions do you work best? Do you function better in the mornings or the evenings? Do you need lots of breaks, or do you work better at a fast pace? When visualizing the ideal environment, think not only of the physical climate but of the emotional and the spiritual ones as well. In what type of setting will you be most able to nurture yourself and, consequently, your clients? How can you put your own unique stamp on your work so that it truly reflects you? What kind of atmosphere do you need so that it most feels like "home"? Visualize your dream environment and make it a reality. DO IT!

How would I describe my ideal work environment?

CHAPTER 6

Do What You Love, the Money Will Follow

Follow your bliss.

—Joseph Campbell

Take out a sheet of paper and divide it into two columns. At the top of the first column, write "Things I Love To Do." At the top of the second column write "How I Spend My Time." Now list the activities that matter to you and that you enjoy under the first heading and the activities that you are currently engaged in under the second. If the two columns don't correspond to a large extent, you should be making some changes. Scrutinizing the fit between the two columns will give you an idea of the degree and the kind of changes you need to make. As you look at your lists, you will notice two types of activities: work-related and non–work related. Although it is sometimes difficult to separate the two, this chapter will focus primarily on work-related activities. Subsequent chapters will address the latter.

Do What You Love, the Money Will Follow. The message in the title of this popular book by Marsha Sinetar (1987) has worked for me and countless others. Before I went into private practice, I was fortunate to have been employed in work settings where I was given the freedom to pursue my interests and, to a large extent, create my own job. Within a broad job description, I was able to pursue the activities I enjoyed and to try out new ones. So if I wanted to do a workshop on a specific area, start a group, do research, write, supervise, or teach—none of which were specifically part of my formal job description—I went ahead and did those activities. It didn't really matter how I spent my time; I got a salary anyhow. Consequently, I learned to create my jobs. I experimented, tried new programs, and generally did what I loved. I approached each new task or project from the standpoint of what would be most fun to do—yes, fun. Making a living was seldom part of the equation because I was getting a steady salary. Unfortunately, many therapists today are unable to enjoy the same conditions, particularly in this harsh economic environment, when organizations are downsizing and adding more work pressures.

I have tried to carry the same attitude into private practice—to choose activities I enjoyed, regardless of their money-making potential, even in the changing economy. For example, even though teaching, doing research, or writing are not as lucrative as seeing clients for therapy, I have always made time for those. Whenever I have a new idea for a project, I will go ahead and do it, whether it generates income or not. Some years ago, I wanted to teach a particular course at a community college. It involved a tremendous time commitment, including course preparation, time in the classroom, traveling back and forth, and so on. Community colleges are not notorious for paying part-time faculty well—at least, not in Arizona. I calculated that I was probably making 50 cents an hour and probably losing money as well, because I was using time in which I could be scheduling therapy appointments to do the class. Although teaching the course made no sense from a financial standpoint, the intellectual and emotional rewards were immense. You cannot put a price tag on enjoyment, learning, or enthusiasm. Of course, you have to look at your own situation and weigh the monetary risks.

When you are doing something you like, its effects will seep into the other areas of your life, even if you are working long hours. In a study comparing two types of workaholics, the enthusiastic workaholics—those who enjoyed their work—experienced more life satisfaction than nonenthusiastic workaholics (Bonebright, Clay, & Ankenmann, 2000). As you might expect, *all* workaholics, whether they enjoyed their work or not, had more work–life conflict than did nonworkaholics and could benefit from learning to get a life outside of work, the topic of the next chapter.

How can you go about creating your dream job? How do you make the things you love to do match the way you spend your time? Go back and review your two lists. How can you make the correspondence between the two columns greater? You may or may not be able to make changes right away, but the suggestions in the rest of the chapter can help you move toward doing what you love.

If You Can't Do It All, Make *Some* Time for What You Love

If you can't do everything you want to completely, see if you can make some time for the things you love to do. If you enjoy writing, for example, but can't afford to leave your job to do that full time, carve out a morning or a day each week to do that. The same goes for any other activity you would like to do but don't feel you have the time for. If you want to spend more time with your children, figure out how you can come home earlier to be with them. If you want to learn Spanish, cooking, filmmaking, or fishing, free up a morning or an evening each week, and sign up for a class. You get the idea. You don't need to do the activity full time. Just make *some* time for it. Don't aim for all-or-nothing behaviors. If you set small, realistic, easily achieved goals, you are more likely to carry them out (Burns, 1980).

If you love to do something that is not revenue producing, begin to do it anyway. You may even want to start a small business using your talents. Nina, a single mother, is an example of that. She had a job that she liked as a therapist in a hospital and that she needed in order to support herself. She also had a talent for writing poetry and for interior design. Nina made time to compose lyrics and, through word of mouth, people started commissioning her to produce poems for special occasions. Even though she hardly made a living from those, she was doing what she loved. She also carved out a few hours in her schedule to take a correspondence course in design and to do some part-time work for an interior decorator.

Make a few activities the mainstay of income generation, and do others just for fun. In an ideal world, all work-related activities would be both satisfying and revenue producing. That, of course, is not always the case. In those situations, let a few of your services generate most of the income. This will allow you the freedom to pursue other projects that you love, which may not be so lucrative. Make time for the things that you enjoy doing, whether you view them as a vocation or an avocation.

Play, Play, Play!

For Nina, creating a poem was play—she enjoyed it, had fun with it, and spent lots of time puttering with it. Playing—on and off the job—brings newness, enthusiasm, and energy to your life and your work. The counterpart of play is what I sometimes refer to as doing "factory work." When I feel stale, am bored with what I'm doing, or find myself merely going through the motions, I know it is time to try something new or to bring some freshness to the situation. Factory work is when you are doing the same thing over and over in the same predictable manner, so that there is no fun, no challenge, and no enjoyment to it. It is when you are putting in your time just to earn a paycheck. Fortunately, in a field where you are working with people, you will always have unpredictability and newness—and room for learning. Work should not be something you force on yourself but, rather, a vehicle for expressing your most positive emotions and talents. When what you do gives you pleasure, you see it as play. You are drawn to it and are energized by it (Ackerman, 1999).

Take Intelligent Risks, and Plan To Succeed

If the thought of doing what you love is scary, I am not suggesting jumping in headfirst but taking intelligent risks and planning for success.

When a system I was working in turned toxic almost overnight, much as I wanted to, I didn't just get up and leave right away. I still had a mortgage, bills, and other expenses to take care of. Instead, I looked at my expenses, estimated what I'd need to make to survive, and figured out that if I had just a small number of clients each week, I could manage. Within a few months, I left my job and started a private practice. Although it didn't offer the safety of a regular paycheck, it feels much safer because my security is within myself, rather than at the whims of other people. Planning was a big part of the process—and planning to succeed. Decide how much of a chance you are willing to take, and maximize the odds of winning. Take a calculated, intelligent risk, and mentally rehearse and visualize what you would like to happen. If the gamble seems too large for a drastic move, figure out how to minimize it or how to take little steps toward your goal. Did I feel trepidation when I took the plunge to move into an environment that suited me? Yes, but so did almost every therapist I have talked to who decided to start his or her own practice. Yet with careful planning and taking measured risks, they made their dream happen.

As I related in the previous chapter, a few years ago I saw several mental health professionals for counseling, mostly for issues related to very unhappy work situations. Each therapist independently decided to leave and start his or her own practice, and today all of these clinicians are thriving—emotionally and financially. "I'm happier than I've ever been," "I love going to work," "It feels so *right.*" Over and over, they'd make statements like these. When they allowed themselves to move to an environment that allowed them to express themselves fully—one where they felt respected and in charge—it is not surprising that they succeeded.

Don't be afraid to take risks. Every time I have taken a chance and deleted an activity I didn't enjoy doing, something else turned up to replace it. This experience has also been true for my colleagues who were afraid to let go. Holding on to something "safe" precludes you from making time for something better. The biggest safety is when you learn that what you have inside you gives you security in the long run.

Focus on How To Make Your Dream Job Happen versus Worrying about How It Can't

Bill's dream was to take long vacations every summer and spend them at the beach. When an opportunity presented itself where he could spend 2 months away doing just that, he immediately started to worry about what that would do to his practice: "What if I lose all my clients?" "What if I won't be able to afford it?" "What if . . . what if . . . what if . . . ?" I suggested to Bill that he *plan* for how he could go away for the summer, instead of engaging in senseless worrying. "You're not planning—you're catastrophizing! What can you do to keep your clients? What kind of arrangements can you make to afford to take the summer off?" Bill quickly saw what he was doing and shifted his mind-set on how to make his dream happen, rather than needlessly fantasizing about all the things that could go wrong. He started making concrete plans to save for it and to prepare his clients. When taking any new step, visualize it, rehearse it, plan it, and *make it happen!*

Have Faith in Yourself and Associate with People Who Have Faith in You

Probably the biggest factor in creating your dream job is having faith in yourself. It is only natural to feel fear and trepidation when starting something new or letting go of something familiar. However, you didn't get this far in life by not trusting in your abilities and resources. Believe in yourself—that's all the security you need. If you like what you do, if you do it well, then people will think of you and refer to you when they need that service. Your enjoyment in your work will enable you to create more opportunities for others to see the value in it. As Martha Sinetar says, "The salesman who loves his products sells these to those with a superior level of interest than the one who is half-heartedly involved with this product" (p. 37).

If you love your work, you'll do it well. Conversely, if you are just doing "factory work" and going through the motions, that will show, too. Studies have shown that a focus on extrinsic rewards can undermine the quality of your work. In a study of creative writers, those who said they wrote primarily for the money did significantly less creative work than those who wrote because of the inner pleasure they got from writing (Amabile, 1985). Other research sugggests that doing something primarily for external rewards can even undermine the natural enjoyment that people originally feel when they are working on tasks of their choosing (Deci, 1975).

Associate with people who have faith in you, and stay away from negative people. It is difficult enough getting rid of the negative tapes playing in your own head without hearing them from others. Hang in there, and remind yourself that if you are doing what you love, most other things fall into place.

Operate from Confidence Rather Than from Fear and Insecurity

If you go *toward* what you want, toward something positive, you will use your inner resourcefulness to make what you want happen. If you operate out of fear and insecurity, you will make the wrong decisions. I will discuss dealing with financial insecurity later on in the book. I have seen many talented young people with a love for music, drawing, acting, or any number of artsy professions major in a "back-up" field such as nursing, education, or law in case they didn't succeed as artists. The implicit message is you can't make money doing what you love—you have to earn your income elsewhere. What happens to these people? You guessed it! They "back up" to their safe, steady jobs because they don't believe they can make it otherwise. Conversely, I have seen many artists doing exactly what they want to—they have not allowed themselves room for a back-up or failure plan. They may not be making as much money as they would if they were in law or medicine—*but they are doing what they love,* and they have a roof over their heads and meals on the table. Again, allow yourself to hang in there, and let your natural talents, assets, and passions dictate how you spend your time.

Calculate the Emotional Rewards in Doing What You Love

"Can I afford to spend my time doing exactly what I want?" you might ask. Can you afford *not* to? Use another measure of success, not just financial, to make a cost-benefit analysis of doing what you love. Value what you've created and look at your inner wealth, which cannot be measured in dollars and cents. Learn to see your work as more than earning a living but as putting what you love and value into your life. As Kahlil Gibran so beautifully put it, "Work is love made visible" (1978, p. 28).

This chapter has been primarily about doing what you enjoy at work. Your job, however, is only part of your total life. The next chapter will focus on how to make room for non–work related activities as well, to maximize the emotional rewards in your life in general, not just in your profession—in short, how to get a life!

Self-Assessment

Review the two lists you made:

Things I Love To Do	*How I Spend My Time*

How closely does the way I spend my time correspond with the activities I enjoy doing?

If they don't match exactly, what changes do I need to make so that the correspondence between the two colums is greater?

Which changes can I make right away?

Which may require more time and planning?

What steps do I need to take to make these changes?

Which suggestions in this chapter would be helpful for me?

_____ If you can't do it all, make *some* time for what you love.

_____ Play, play, play!

_____ Take intelligent risks and plan to succeed.

_____ Focus on how you can make your dream job happen versus worrying about how it can't.

_____ Have faith in yourself, and associate with people who have faith in you.

_____ Operate from confidence, rather than from fear and insecurity.

_____ Calculate the emotional rewards in doing what you love.

CHAPTER 7

Get a Life

You just need to get a life, a real life, a full life, a professional life, yes, but another life, too.
—Anna Quindlen, *A Short Guide to a Happy Life*

Although very few therapists go into the mental health profession because of the money (as my good friend, a retired psychologist, likes to say, go to plumbing school if you want to get rich), for some people economics frequently play a role in their not having a life outside of work. More often than not, however, it isn't mere finances but the feeling that one has to be productive at all times that keeps many practitioners from taking the time for other hobbies, leisure activities, or just lounging around and "doing nothing." Even therapists who give lip service to the importance of "down" time and "balance" in life—and prescribe those for their clients—do not always practice what they preach (Kottler, 1993), at least not without a twinge of guilt—particularly those who are in private practice, where "time is money."

"I'd love to take a yoga class, but it's on Wednesday mornings, and that's 3 client hours."

"I'd like to have lunch with my friends more regularly, but I can't afford to take off 2 hours every week to do that."

"When I retire, I'm going to learn Spanish. I'd love to do that now, but I don't have the time."

"I'm going to have to cancel our lunch because I just got a new referral."

"I want to take up scuba diving, but I have so much work to do now, I don't know where I'd fit it in."

"I'd love to be able to take a month off, but I'm worried that I'll lose all of my clients if I do that."

"It's true that I'm working very hard right now and that I don't have time for all the things I want to do, but I'm building a nest egg so that when I retire, I will be comfortable. Then I will have time for all the things I want to do."

"I wish I could have dinner with my family every night, but I have to work several evenings a week because that's the only time my clients can come."

Can you identify, even a tiny bit, with any of these statements? It's easy to look at other people who work a ridiculous number of hours and call them "workaholics," "driven," or any number of descriptive labels. Even if you are not a workaholic yourself, you probably feel a twinge of guilt when you cut out an activity that is "revenue producing" or "productive" and substitute it with one that is not. However, you may have to do just that to make time for the life you want—time for the activities you put on your list in the previous chapter, those activities that give you joy and that you love doing.

Having a full life outside of work is necessary for self-renewal, and experts recommend that as health professionals, we intentionally make time for activities that replenish us, from gardening to going to concerts, to playing ball. What's more, they encourage early training for psychotherapists to develop relaxation habits and to pursue them with the same commitment and energy that they do their work (Ziegler & Kanas, 1986).

Your Money or Your Life?

If "time is money," how do you make time for all those things that don't make money? Joe Dominguez and Vicki Robin, in their book *Your Money or Your Life* (1999), suggest looking at the "life cost" of some of the activities you are doing, how much "life" is needed to be exchanged for the work. Do a cost-benefit analysis of each task you are engaged in, not just in terms of its monetary value, but also of its emotional cost. Calculate which ones are worth keeping and which you want to get rid of. Although the authors provide a fairly complicated formula to determine the true value of what you are actually making per hour (hint: by the time you deduct taxes, overhead, wear and tear, travel time, and so on, it's a fraction of what you think) and give you an idea of how many hours in life units it is costing you to, say, upgrade your car (a lot!), you do not necessarily need a statistical equation to do a cost-benefit analysis. For each hour of work, try to determine how much it is giving you in terms of "money" and how much you are giving up in terms of "life": your money or your life. Don't be surprised if what you are actually getting in dollars and cents is, in most cases, only roughly a third of what you *think* you are making after subtracting expenses. Ask yourself, for example: How much extra money am I actually making when I work 3 evenings a week? What is it actually costing me in terms of stress, health, family relationships—life? Is it worth it?

"Can I afford to give up those things that are preventing me from having a life?" you might ask. The real question is, "Can you afford not to?" Take a good look at how you are spending your time. If you have no room in your schedule for the things you love to do, if you are constantly waiting for retirement or "some day" to make time for the things you enjoy, then you can't afford *not* to have a life.

In fact, if you want to be effective and happy in your job, it is of utmost importance to get a life outside of your professional one. A study of passionately committed psychotherapists, those who were energized and invigorated by their work, instead of being drained by it, and who continued to thrive and love it, in spite of obstacles, suggests a reciprocal relationship between passion for life and passion for work (Dlugos & Friedlander, 2001). The authors of this research conclude that sustaining passionate commitment to work as a psychotherapist reflects commitment in other areas of life. By engaging in other activities that supply them with energy, therapists are able to work more efficiently and enjoy their jobs more. Being emotionally available to clients may be dependent on being more alive generally. In interviews with clinicians who were nominated by their peers as being most passionately committed, everyone in the sample said that attending to his or her nonprofessional life was essential to maintaining passion and avoiding burnout. Those therapists maintained very strict boundaries between their personal and professional lives, took vacations frequently, and even changed work settings to have the flexibility to attend to other areas of life. In addition, almost all of them mentioned at least one nonprofessional activity with as much passion as they had when speaking about work.

The most interesting finding was that *work is not the primary commitment in the lives of therapists who are considered to be passionately committed to their work.* They ranked work only third among the five life roles of participation, fifth for commitment, and fourth for expectations of satisfaction. In other words, work was not their most significant priority. The data suggest that passionate commitment to work does not mean overcommitment to work. Indeed, the therapists expressed the view that their effectiveness would be diminished if they did not make deliberate efforts to prevent their work from intruding into their personal lives.

What does this mean for you? It means that to maintain passion as a psychotherapist, you have to balance your life with other activities, even if that requires reducing work hours, passing up opportunities for advancement, or changing jobs. When it comes to "your money" or "your life," you have to invest in your life to be a more passionate, more effective, and happier therapist. You have to get a full life, a balanced one, one where you put at least as much energy into the activities outside of your professional life as into those within it. As we saw in the last chapter, even workaholics who enjoy their work have more conflicts than do their nonworkaholic counterparts and need to learn a better work–life balance (Bonebright, Clay, & Ankenmann, 2000).

How Much Is Enough?

Only you can answer that question, but many people who have decided to put a cap on their working hours found that they were more than able to make ends meet by making a few simple adjustments. Dr. Janet Pipal (1997), a licensed psychologist who lectures on "Private Practice Sanity," gave numerous examples of this at a workshop, one of which particularly stood out for me. She related that prior to leaving managed care, she was too stressed and tired to cook and frequently ate out, spending quite a bit of money on restaurant meals. Now she enjoys cooking and eating dinner at home. There are innumerable "costs" in not having a life, the least of which are monetary.

Other therapists, writing on their own and others' self-care, have also stressed the importance of giving yourself permission not to earn so much money. Michael Mahoney (1997) writes that allowing himself to earn less than his colleagues, many of whom made nearly three times as much as he did, has made a significant difference in his enjoyment of life. Arnold Lazarus (2000), in his advice to clinicians on replenishing themselves, puts it this way: "A basic goal in my life has never been to make money—only to earn a decent living. Therein lies my perception of psychological nourishment. My bank account may have suffered but my psyche has been enriched" (p. 93). How much is enough? You'd be surprised!

Think Downsizing, Instead of Upsizing

When making your cost-benefit analysis, look carefully at all of your expenses. How much do you really need? How much can you cut out? Look at your budget and activities in the same manner that you would look at your closet to weed out any clothes that you don't need any longer, and then purge any extra expenses. Freeing yourself up financially gives you more time for the things you enjoy. Now look at the activities that you engage in—just as with your clothes, keep only those that you love and need. Get rid of the rest!

Elaine St. James, in her book *Simplify Your Life* (1994), gives some very good suggestions on minimizing expenses to give you more time to enjoy your life. These include living on less than you earn, rethinking your buying habits, and reducing your needs for goods and services, among others. Another book with excellent tips for cutting costs is *The 50 Best Ways to Simplify Your Life* (2001) by Patrick Fanning and Heather Garnos Mitchener. The authors give practical hints on breaking the money habit, shopping smart and simple, investing wisely, and other tips to help you downsize. Although this chapter is not so much about how to reduce expenses, the general idea is to think in terms of trimming your budget so that you can have more *time,* rather than increasing your work hours to make more *money,* which in the long run costs you more in life units.

Get a Life NOW!

If you are waiting for retirement or "some day" to make time for the activities you enjoy, it may be too late then. If you are like millions of people who think that you have to sacrifice now to ensure a comfortable retirement, you might take comfort in Ralph Warner's book *Get a Life* (2000), which explodes the myth that you need a great deal of cash to retire well. In fact, the chances of enjoying a satisfying retirement have almost nothing to do with money. Spending all your time working to save for old age—and neglecting family, friends, and health in the process—does not make the way to a blissful retirement. As one retiree told Warner, "If your entire life centers around your work, then your life stops when your work stops" (p. 71).

Of course, planning for the future and putting aside a financial nest egg are important, but overinvesting in dollars and underinvesting in the other factors that make for a fulfilling retirement don't make sense. Rather than spending all your time developing your financial resources for the future, the time would be more wisely spent developing a life apart from work now, to prepare for a life apart from work when work stops.

What makes for a successful retirement? Warner lists several "commodities" to invest in right now. First of all, develop your curiosity. This is the time to learn new skills. If you don't nurture your thirst for knowledge now, what do you think your chances of vegetating are when you are older? Invest in your health. Now is the time to exercise, learn healthy eating habits, or stop smoking. It is wiser to put your time and energy into your physical well-being than to save for a nursing home. Stay physically active. Learn to make new friends of all ages. If you don't take the time to meet friends for lunch, or if you don't have the energy to make new friends, whom will you spend your time with when you retire? The same goes for family. Phyllis Diller used to joke that it is important to be nice to your children because they ultimately decide which nursing home to place you in! Kidding aside, if you don't take the time for children and family now, how can you expect them to be there for you later on? This is particularly true for parents of young children. Take the time *now* to be with them. You will be a therapist forever, a hands-on mom or dad for only a few precious years. Find meaningful interests. The time to take that cooking class, that scuba diving lesson, that woodworking or Spanish course is *now,* not later. You don't need to invest in your financial future as much as in other aspects of life. In short, get a life and get it *now!*

One of my clients, who took a few years off when he was only in his 40s, used to talk about "taking retirement in increments." He didn't want to wait until he was 65 to do what he wanted. Every few years, whenever he could, he'd take a few years off and engage in all those activities he was going to do "some day." I have always liked that phrase, "taking retirement in increments." Injecting small doses of "retirement" into your days is about getting a life now.

Getting ready for retirement is, of course, not the only reason to do the things you want now. However, if telling yourself that this is an investment in your future helps you sign up for that Spanish class, meet a friend for lunch, or go hiking, do it! It doesn't matter what your reasons are for starting your "retirement in increments." Just get a life *now!*

I was talking to a colleague of mine, an energetic, dynamic psychiatrist, who was about to retire after many decades, and I mentioned Warner's book *Get a Life* on preparing for retirement. "I have a life," she countered. She certainly did. She had so many interests and was engaged in so many activities, I wondered when she had time for them. What is noteworthy is that she didn't wait until she stopped working to learn Spanish, travel to far-off places, visit children and grandchildren, read books, compete in swimming tournaments, have an active social life, go to lunch with friends, or participate in any number of other activities. She was engaged, interested, and active—in her outside life and in her work. Her advice for beginning therapists? "Have a *personal* life that is fulfilling, supportive, interesting and that contains 'change of pace' activities."

Getting a life isn't just about investing in a successful retirement or making time for activities you love. It is also giving yourself the time to *enjoy* those moments as they come. As Anna Quindlen says in her book *A Short Guide to a Happy Life* (2000), "Life is made of moments, small pieces of glittering mica in a long stretch of gray cement. It would be wonderful if they came to us unsummoned, but particularly in lives as busy as the ones most of us lead now, that won't happen. We have to teach ourselves how to make room for them, to love them, and to live, really live" (pp. 41–42).

Get a life!

Self-Assessment

Although this exercise may at first seem to be more suited for therapists in private practice, it will still help you even if you are employed full time, particularly if you wish to cut down on your hours or if you are engaged in some extracurricular employment in addition to your regular job. Conduct a cost-benefit analysis for each of the work activities you are currently engaged in. For each hour of work, calculate how much it is giving you in terms of "money" and how much it is costing you in terms of "life." Deduct taxes, overhead, and other incidental expenses to get the true value of your earnings. For each task, ask yourself:

How much money am I actually making per hour when I factor in paperwork, phone calls, travel time, cancellations, no-shows, and so on?

What is it costing me in peace of mind, health, family relationships—"life"?

ACTIVITY	***TRUE HOURLY EARNINGS***	***LIFE COST***
______	______	______
______	______	______
______	______	______
______	______	______

Are there any activities where the monetary benefits are just not worth the cost?

How much is enough?

What are some ways of downsizing? What expenses can I cut down on so that I have more time for the things I enjoy?

What "commodities" can I invest in right now for a successful retirement?

_____ Curiosity

_____ Health

_____ Friends

_____ Family

_____ Interests and hobbies

What concrete steps can I take to do that?

CHAPTER 8

Make Your Calendar Your Most Important Tool

Time is life . . . to master your time is to master your life and make the most of it.

—Alan Lakein, *How to Get Control of Your Time and Your Life*

How do you go about getting a life? Put down those activities that you like on your schedule and eliminate those that drain you. In this and the next chapter, I will discuss making room for the positive activities, and in Chapters 10, 11, and 12, I will elaborate on getting rid of the "energy drainers."

Put It on the Calendar

Just schedule the activities that matter to you on your calendar. Simple? Yes. If something is on your schedule, you will do it. If it's not, it won't get done! Like most working people, you probably rely on an appointment book to keep track of your commitments and where you need to be at a certain time. Woody Allen used to say that much of life is to "just show up," and most of us are conditioned to just show up and be there for whatever it says in our appointment book.

Some years ago, several doctors and I were conducting a workshop for other physicians on improving communication with patients. One of the doctors asked, "How can I build rapport? I don't have the time to spend with every patient addressing his concerns. I only have 15 minutes, and I'm rushing from one patient to another." I will always remember the response of one of the workshop leaders, a well-respected and caring physician: "Who controls your calendar? You can choose to schedule patients every 15 minutes or you can schedule them for a half hour or longer. You have to *choose.*"

This is about choice. We each have the same allotted 24 hours a day, and it is up to us to decide what goes into each hour. The calendar is, of course, the operational definition of how you are spending your time, just as your checkbook is a reflection of how you are spending your money. Look at your appointment book, figure out how you can make time for the activities you would like to do, and schedule them in!

Lois, a therapist with a young daughter, would simply write down her child's name, Elizabeth, in her book the same way she wrote down her clients' names. Another counselor puts down her own name in the spaces and honors her commitment to herself in the same way that she guards appointments with other people. All you have to do is mark down what you will be doing next to the time. It does not have to be an "appointment" with a specific person for it to count. You could list activities, as well as the names of persons. Entries could include "write," "swimming," "paperwork," or any other number of both work and non–work related activities. *If it's not on the calendar, you won't do it.* It's as simple as that.

Heather, a psychologist who had a book contract, was frustrated by her inability to find time to write. She had two children whom she loved to spend time with, as well as a busy practice. She kept hoping for "snatches of time" between her busy job and her home life, in which she could work on her book. Knowing how mentally demanding an activity writing can be, I could tell that she was setting herself up for not fulfilling her contract. If writing the book was important to her, she needed to free up at least a morning or a day each week for writing, and *block off that time.* If you really want to do something, mark it down on your calendar. Don't wait until you are "in the mood" or for when you have "free time" to do it. That won't happen.

Many therapists, like Heather, report that they constantly feel frustrated. They are going from one appointment to another and feel that they have no time to return phone calls, do paperwork, or deal with unexpected events or emergencies. Bob, a therapist, lists a major stress as "returning pages and phone calls and seeing patients with no breaks in-between." In fact, time pressures are very big on the list of therapist stressors (Nash, Norcross, & Prochaska, 1984).

Workload stress can produce signs of disruption in only 20 minutes if it is extreme. In a study where participants had only that much time to respond to memos and letters before going to an important meeting and were constantly interrupted by telephone calls and slow-speaking staff members, they began to exhibit noticeable signs of strain, including motor restlessness, irritability, muttering under their breath, and even swearing at the secretary (Tett, Bobocel, Hafer, Lees, Smith, & Jackson, 1992). If only a few minutes can bring on these symptoms, imagine the consequences of doing that 40 or more hours a week. Schedule breaks before you start yelling at your coworkers!

Many clinicians, like Bob, schedule themselves so tightly that they end up feeling stressed by the "intrusion" of telephone calls, administrative details, and so on. If these are part of the job, schedule time for them so that you won't end up feeling frustrated, like Bob or Heather, at not being able to "fit them in." The same goes for non–work related activities. Penny, a therapist who loves movies and the theater and who values her relationship with her daughters, makes time for both by buying season tickets to shows for her and her children and taking one afternoon off every week to go to the movies with them. She does not wait until she has the time. She simply *makes* the time, putting it down on her calendar and showing up! Even therapists who punch a time clock and do not have as much control over their schedules can make some adjustments and build in breathers.

Create Open Spaces in Your Schedule

I have heard a balanced life be compared to a pie divided into three equal sections: a third for life work, a third for relationships, and a third for "I" time. Although most people do not spend a third of their waking hours in "I" time, many clinicians are even worse. They give themselves very little room for maneuverability. Anita, a graphic artist, discussed the importance of leaving "white spaces" around a design or it will look too cluttered. The same can be said for time. Build some white space into your day to make room for the unexpected and the expected. Julie, a counselor, discovered that when she freed up at least an hour daily, instead of scheduling every hour with clients, she felt rested, relaxed, and not as rushed as she usually did. In addition, she was able to be a more effective therapist because she could give her full attention to her clients, instead of worrying about when she'd do her paperwork or return her calls.

Pacing is very important. Find a rhythm that works for you and work at that pace, rather than pushing yourself. I have heard it said that an optimal pace is one between "rusting out"—too little—and "burning out"—too much (Tubesing, 1978). Figure out what yours is, and plan your day accordingly. Many therapists today, instead of working the traditional 50- to 60-minute hour, with a brief break between clients, are tightening their schedules and putting clients on the calendar every 45 minutes with no breaks in-beween. Of course, they get to see more patients per day—but that takes its toll—on them and on those they treat. Some practitioners routinely go without a break for lunch, at a pace that leaves them tired, hungry, and stressed. If your day is so tightly packed that you don't have room for routine paperwork, as well as the unexpected emergencies, it is important to create white spaces in it.

Create work breaks in your daily routine. Burnout experts recommend the liberal use of these to serve as buffers against stress, giving you time and space to unwind and let off steam (Maslach, 1986). Dr. Raymond Fowler (2000), CEO of the American Psychological Association for 13 years before he retired in 2002, is a strong advocate of building in downtime and stresses that good time management doesn't mean working every possible minute.

Another reason for creating open slots in your schedule is that if you don't have them, then you can't fill them up with the things you love to do. If every minute is structured, there is no room for taking that computer course, going to the gym, sitting in the sun, or anything else you want to do. Make room for the things you like.

Whenever You Add Something to Your Schedule, Subtract Something Else

Once you find a pace or a rhythm that works for you, you may be tempted to fill up your day with more activities. Even if everything on your calendar is important and meaningful, you still have to make choices and prioritize. A useful tip is that any time you want to add something new to your schedule, you need to subtract something. You do this automatically, of course, when you enter in clients' names. You can't fill up your regular Wednesday 10 o'clock appointment, for example, until the client who occupies that slot terminates and you can give the hour to someone else. With activities that are not so structured or clear-cut, you may be tempted to take on more projects without clearing your calendar of other commitments first. If you do that, you'll have another load in addition to your regular work. Heather is a good example of someone who tried to add writing a book to her already-busy schedule, without making room for it first—with predictable results. Don't take on new projects, thinking you'll "fit them in." Make room for them by clearing the space first. For every project you take on, take out something else.

You Can Do It All, Just Not All at Once

When Heather looked at her already-busy schedule, she realized that she realistically didn't have time to free up a morning or two a week to write her book and meet the deadline—at least, not this year. Yes, she could spend less time with her children, but she chose not to—at least, not for now. She decided that finishing the book was not a priority for her at this time in her life. She was going to be moving to another city in a few months and was already planning to pare down her practice. As she freed up her workload, she would then be able to make room for her writing.

It is possible to do it all, just not all at once. A corollary of that is take on only one major project at a time. Wait until the task is completed before starting a new one. You may be tempted to do too many activities, all of which you love, but you may end up feeling tired and frazzled. Lisa, for example, was starting a new program at work that required a great deal of energy on her part. She also needed to take a certification exam, which would give her more flexibility at work. Both the program and the exam were important to her. Just as Heather did, however, she decided to wait until one project was firmly in place before she undertook another major task that required much energy. It is well known that the more life changes occur to you at a given time (even good ones!), the more prone to stress and illness you become (Holmes & Masuda, 1974). It makes sense to take on only one major project or activity at a time, no matter how stimulating, positive, and rewarding it is. Otherwise, you'll bite off more than you can chew.

This chapter has focused mainly on how to make time for the things that matter to you. The next chapter will further elaborate on this theme—how to add more positive activities to your schedule.

Self-Assessment

Look at your schedule the way you would look at a budget. How can you make room for the things that matter and cut down on the energy-draining activities that deplete you?

What positive activities do I need to put on my calendar?

What energy-draining activities do I need to clear out to make room for these?

Where can I build more "white spaces" into my calendar?

CHAPTER 9

Diversify, Diversify, Diversify

Variety is the very spice of life.
—William Cowper

In the previous chapter, I talked about the necessity—for you and for your clients—of making room in your schedule for activities you enjoy. I stressed the importance of having a balanced life in general. This chapter is about having balance *within* your professional life. How can you fill up your work life with activities that stimulate and renew you, that continually recharge your batteries? One of the practitioner-tested, research-informed strategies for successful therapist self-care is diversity and synergy of professional activities (Norcross, 2000). This means having a lot of variety in what you do when you are at work. No matter how much you love your job, if you are doing the same thing, day in and day out, without any change, eventually, you will hit a plateau. Work will seem stale and routine at best—and boring and aversive at worst. Depending on the complexity of the job, it takes 3 to 5 years for the sense of mastery and challenge to be replaced by a feeling of boredom if the work remains the same (Bardwick, 1988). So if you have been doing the same thing over and over for the last 3 years, you are very likely to have the plateau doldrums. If you want to remain fully involved and energized—for yourself and for your clients—having constant change and new learning is essential.

"I just can't concentrate on what my client is saying."

"I keep watching the clock till the session is over."

"This is so easy, I could do it with my eyes closed."

"Once you've seen one eating disorder client (alcoholic, angry teen, depressed mother . . . etc., etc.), they all start to sound alike."

"I don't find doing therapy as exhilarating as I used to."

"I don't think I can do this for the rest of my life."

"If I have to listen to one more client talking about her depression (anxiety, marriage, etc., etc.), I will throw up."

If you find yourself having feelings like this, don't panic. It just means you have reached a plateau and need more diversity and stimulation in your work. Do you recall the emotions you had when you started a work activity for the first time—the anticipation, the nervousness, and the thrill of doing something that you had never done before? Some beginning therapists even compare it to the sensations of first love. It is new, exciting, different—everything about it is stimulating. You can't get enough of it. Then the novelty wears off, it becomes more routine, even dull for some people. This is called plateauing. The initial high lasts for a short time, followed by a period where "a job is a job is a job." Most people plateau after 3 years of doing the same thing. How can you continue to add enthusiasm and spark to your job? In order for you to continue to grow both personally and professionally, new learning must continually take place. Let's explore some strategies to diversify your professional life and keep it interesting.

Engage in Many Forms of Therapy with Different Types of Patients and Problems

Even if you spend most of your day doing therapy, you can vary your work by doing different forms of therapy. In addition to individual counseling, you can see couples or families together. This certainly requires a different mind-set and way of working and can easily break the pattern of seeing client after client. Group therapy is another form of treatment that provides a change of pace and keeps you out of the rut of meeting with one person after another. Engaging in multiple types of therapy disrupts the tempo and adds variety and newness to your job. Not every therapist is comfortable working with couples, families, or groups, however. It is important that you explore the options that best suit your unique strengths or comfort level. Even if you choose to do only individual therapy, break up the monotony by switching chairs.

The diversity in orientation can also provide much-needed stimulation. Although you may be committed to one school of thought, having an "arsenal of tricks," as one of my friends put it, helps get you out of a predictable routine. Espousing an eclectic theoretical orientation not only allows you to adapt the way you work to your client's needs, it also provides diversity. I am most energized when I find myself using different types of skills and therapies in one day, ranging from behavioral to psychodynamic. In the course of a few hours, I may be alternating between teaching a mother parenting skills, exploring the significance of a dream, actively mediating between members of a couple, or merely providing a client a safe place to cry.

You can also shift gears by working with many types of clients and problems. Some therapists burn out because they specialize in one area, get pegged as an expert in that field, and soon start getting referrals only in their specialty. Although you may have one or several areas of expertise, it is still important not to allow yourself to be pigeonholed and, consequently, end up limiting yourself to one type of patient or problem. Irvin Yalom, a therapist for 4 decades, in his book *The Gift of Therapy* (2002), states that therapist demoralization occurs if he or she overspecializes, especially in areas filled with great pain, such as dying patients or severely psychotic ones. In his advice to therapists, he recommends balance and diversity in their practice to contribute to a sense of renewal.

A friend of mine has two offices on opposite sides of town, where the clientele in each location is strikingly different, reflecting the demographics of the two geographical areas. In one place, she sees mainly blue-collar workers and in the other wealthy, educated, upper-middle-class executives. The contrast between the two settings keeps her consistently stimulated. Besides socioeconomic status, you can see clients of various ages and types of problems.

Many therapists speak about their professional renewal as a result of doing psychotherapy with diverse clinical populations. Some practitioners may do that automatically when they change jobs and work in a different setting. If you are in private practice, however, you may have to actively seek out new types of clients. Working part time in another environment, volunteering at an agency, or doing a few hours of pro bono work are some ways that clinicians have added variety to their professional lives.

Participate in a Variety of Work Activities

"I could never be a therapist. I can't imagine spending all day every day listening to people's problems," I'm often told. "How do you do it?" The answer is, I don't. Psychotherapy is only one of the many activities that clinicians do, and you can add diversity in your day by alternating between those. Whenever I am asked what I like about psychology, I usually mention the variety of things to do within the field: psychotherapy, assessment, research, teaching, supervision, consulting, public speaking, administration, or program planning. These are only for starters! The number of tasks you can engage in is limited only by your imagination.

Professionals who are most satisfied with their work are those who don't have to do therapy full time—for example, academics or administrators (Norcross & Guy, 1989). They have a great deal of control over how many clients they wish to see and when. Although therapists in full-time practice may not have as much leeway as these workers, they can still employ some diversity in their work activities. As Morris Eagle (2001), a psychologist and a psychodynamic therapist for over 40 years, states, "I cannot imagine, unless my livelihood entirely depended on it, doing psychotherapy on a full-time basis. I do not think that I could or would be an effective therapist under those circumstances. I often wonder how therapists who handle 40 or more patient hours per week can be effective. I know that I could not be" (p. 37).

The research bears this out. As I mentioned in Chapter 4, it is not the number of working hours that leads to burnout but the amount of direct contact with patients or clients (Maslach, 1982). When I asked therapists how many clients they could comfortably see per week without getting burned out, not one clinician came close to 40 hours. Responses ranged from 15 to 30, with only one person saying 35. When asked what they considered the *optimal* number of client hours per week, their responses ranged from 10 to 30, with most therapists feeling that 15 to 20 hours were ideal. Although the majority of practitioners can only handle 20 or so clients per week, many fill up their schedules with therapy appointments, depleting themselves and robbing their patients of their effective presence. If you are feeling less than engaged, responsive, and energized in your sessions, it is time to introduce some different activities into your schedule. Diversify. Don't put all your eggs into one basket!

Combine What You Love with Professional Activities

Harry is the prototype of a Renaissance man. A caring and committed psychotherapist, he also has numerous other interests. He is a talented musician and spent much of his early years pursuing music while working as a clinician. In later years, he has focused on photography and painting and spends half his week seeing clients and the other half pursuing his art, which he has displayed in galleries and art shows.

Jean is a gifted actress and comedienne. She is also a psychotherapist. She combines her love for acting with her love of mental health by conducting workshops on the use of humor. Her colleague, who also has a knack for acting, makes use of psychodrama in her work and directs young people in performances on various psychological topics.

Mark melds his education in psychology with his passion for politics. He is active in legislation and has been instrumental in promoting several mental health bills. He thrives on the ins and outs of the legislature and uses his knowledge of mental health to bring about change.

Nina brings her love of poetry into her work. She frequently makes rhymes about her clients and uses those in therapy. She also writes poems about various important mental health issues, some of which have been read at national conferences.

Lottie mixes her love for film and her love for psychology by writing and producing videos on all manner of psychotherapy themes.

David, a self-described computer nerd, spends much of his time writing computer programs covering a potpourri of mental health topics. He also incorporates his love of computers into other aspects of his work, whether it is creating a billing system or exploring doing therapy on the Internet.

Leslie, who majored in both creative writing and psychology in college, uses both of her interests in her work. She loves to write, whether she is preparing a speech or authoring an article or a book.

There are so many ways to incorporate your talents and your skills into your work, providing you with the variety and the diversity to constantly stay fresh and responsive to your clients. If you feel like you want to do something different, brainstorm on how you can bring in something new to your job and how you can combine it with your hobbies and interests.

Continually Pursue New Learning

Studies indicate that happy, involved, and energized therapists frequently use teaching, studying, supervising, and consulting to keep themselves attuned to new ways of thinking about their work (Ronnestad & Skovholt, 2001). Constantly learning new skills and approaches is stimulating in and of itself. Most mental health professionals I talked to stressed the importance of new learning in helping them stay enthusiastic and involved in their interactions with those they treat. Learning, much like psychotherapy, is a process and not an end product. It helps you see your clients in novel ways, whether you learn from workshops or from your mistakes. Continued education keeps you enthusiastic, engaged, and interested—all of which are essential in dealing with your clients. Fortunately, there are many formal opportunities to pick up new information. Therapists stressed the importance of taking advantage of continuing education opportunities to rejuvenate themselves. Reading, taking classes, and engaging in dialogue with colleagues are other avenues for increasing your knowledge.

Of course, most of the learning takes place from the people you treat. I have learned more about human behavior and psychotherapy from my clients than I have from textbooks. It may be a cliché, but my clients are my best teachers. As many clinicians state, in one form or another, one of the greatest rewards in being a therapist is their own personal growth, in terms of their patients' educating them.

Not only do your clients teach you about life, you invariably learn lessons in areas you may not have an opportunity to experience otherwise. You can learn the intimate details of the life of a flight attendant, a physician, or a carpet layer. You learn about the ins and outs of corporations, politics, and educational institutions. You learn about different cultures and religious groups. You learn the secret concerns of adolescents and older people. You learn about new restaurants, jazz bands, hiking trails, and vacation spots. You learn about new things every day, and the more you diversify, the more you learn.

Diversify, diversify, diversify!

Self-Assessment

Which of these suggestions can I utilize to diversify my work?

_____ Engage in multiple forms of therapy with different types of patients' behaviors.

_____ Participate in a variety of work activities.

_____ Combine what I love with professional activities.

_____ Continually pursue new learning.

CHAPTER 10

Simplify, Simplify, Simplify

Wise men and women in every major culture throughout history have found that the secret to happiness is not in getting more but in wanting less.

—Elaine St. James, *Simplify Your Life*

The preceding chapters have focused largely on adding activities to your days to live the way you want. The next three deal with eliminating those things that bring on stress. This chapter is about uncluttering your world of things that drain you, to give you time for the balanced, rewarding life you deserve. If you feel that you have no time or energy to do the things you enjoy, you are not alone. Time pressures, an excessive workload, and a sense of enormous responsibility are three of the most frequently endorsed occupational hazards for therapists (Kramen-Kahn & Hansen, 1998). Fully 68% of psychologists in clinical practice listed "too much paperwork" and "inadequate time for all obligations" as causing distress or impairment (Sherman & Thelen, 1998). The increasing demands from the changing health environment have resulted in more time pressures and obligations, with insurance companies requiring therapists to document their work with clients in excruciating detail. Modern technology has added to the time urgency, with beepers, e-mails, fax machines, and cellular phones constantly taking up precious minutes. Many clinicians work at home, where the computer is going, or they try to do their endless paperwork or return phone calls when they should be relaxing. They lead a frenetic life, which can be a major cause of burnout (Grosch & Olsen, 1994). Time pressures affect not only clinicians, but their families as well. Although most children of therapists feel that certain of their parents' skills, such as empathy and tolerance, may be helpful for them, children decry the long hours that their parents work and the occasional intrusions of patients into their home lives (Golden & Farber, 1998).

How can you simplify your life and declutter it from the things that you don't want to do, to leave room for the things that matter? How can you make time to enhance your life and that of your family? In this chapter, I would like to offer some practical, concrete, and specific suggestions that have worked for me and others, to help you do just that. Although some of these ideas may be more relevant for a private practice than for an agency setting, where you may not have as much flexibility, many of the hints can be applied regardless of what type of environment you work in. Some of these tips save you time, some save you money, some save you paperwork, and all save you stress.

Engage in Low-Maintenance Living at Home and at Work

I will mainly focus on ways to simplify your life at work. For suggestions on how to unclutter your life in general, I urge you to pick up Elaine St. James's book *Simplify Your Life* (1994) or Patrick Fanning and Heather Garnos Mitchener's book *The 50 Best Ways to Simplify Your Life* (2001), both of which I referred to in Chapter 7. Each book provides numerous ideas on slowing down and enjoying the things that matter to you, and you will no doubt derive some useful hints that you can apply to your life, from building a simple wardrobe to reducing the amount of junk in your home.

To make your life as maintenance-free as possible, look at each task you undertake and ask yourself how important it is, whether it needs to get done, and whether there are ways of making it simpler and less time-consuming. As you cut down on activities that are unimportant or unnecessary, you automatically make more room for the ones that mean a lot to you. The events that take up your waking moments could range from household chores to social engagements to business-related responsibilities. If you are spending hours on meaningless tasks and have no time for the things that nourish you, figure out how to stop doing those nonessential activities—or, at least, minimize how long you work on them. If you are, for example, using up a large chunk of your day traveling to and from work or between settings, you might decide to do what Larry did, by moving closer to his job; as Linda did by going to the office only 3 days a week and doing her paperwork at home; or by keeping only one office instead of working at several places, as Jeanne decided to do.

Don't just get rid of unnecessary activities; throw out nonessential objects as well, which only make it more difficult for you to function. The fewer things there are around you, the less you have to take care of. If you haven't used something in a year or two, dispose of it. Having a clutter-free house or desk helps with the mental clutter as well. Papers, knickknacks, and other items that take up lots of space are constant reminders of what needs to be done, and they use up valuable mental and physical energy—time and energy that could be spent on activities that you want to do.

One of the first things you can do to simplify your work life is to start cutting back on the number of hours you spend at your job. If you are not self-employed, explore the possibility with your supervisor of reducing your work hours. When my son was little, I did just that and went from working 40 to 32 hours a week. I was able to keep my benefits, and the loss in pay was barely noticeable. However, the rewards of being able to have more time with my child were huge. When I went into private practice, I had even more freedom to cut back on my work hours. Many therapists who work in the public sector have been able to cut down on their work hours without too many problems. In fact, a few reported that their employers were often happy to save on the expenses! However, if you are a sole provider, you may not always be able to do so in today's economic climate. Furthermore, there may be other repercussions, such as your supervisor not considering you a "serious" employee. Only you can evaluate your own particular situation and decide on the pros and cons. The cost-benefit analysis in the previous chapter can be very helpful in this regard.

If you are working for yourself, schedule your day to start an hour later (or to end an hour earlier). You may be amazed at how easy that is to do and what little difference it will make in terms of productivity or income. You will be pleasantly surprised at what a remarkable boon it can be to your energy level and overall well-being. If it is difficult for you to immediately implement this change, do it an hour at a time. When a slot is freed up after a client terminates, do not schedule anyone else for that time—keep it free. Gradually, cut back on your work hours until you are spending only 20 to 25 hours a week "at work." Remember, this is within the range that most therapists whom I surveyed said was ideal for them. This gives you room for other things, and monetarily, it can be more than enough as well. The 20 to 25 hours (or whatever number is best for you) should also include paperwork, phone calls, and other non–revenue producing activities. I will discuss finances and downsizing later in the chapter. Your optimal number of hours may be more or less than 20 to 25. It is not just the number of hours but how you feel about them. For example, doctors who worked longer hours because they *wanted* to reported significantly less burnout that those who worked the same amount of hours but preferred to work less (Barnett & Hyde, 2001). Whatever number you pick, cut back on your work hours until you reach it. The ideal schedule for you is when you have time to do all the other things you want.

One way to work less and enjoy it more is to give up the busy work. When people have set hours when they must be at work, many of them manage to fill up their day with unnecessary activities, such as making unneeded phone calls, dealing with interruptions, engaging in chit-chat, getting another cup of coffee, attending meetings, or any number of things that take up time and that do not necessarily need to be done. Somehow, people use up the time. Giving up the distractions will make your work day more satisfying because you'll be spending it only on activities that matter and doing what you really want to do.

Go to work with a specific list of what you wish to accomplish that day, and leave when you have completed those tasks. Don't get sidetracked into doing other things. Make your list as *brief* and *realistic* as possible. If you constantly have 20 things on your to-do list and accomplish only 2 or 3, you will just end up frustrated. If you keep looking at the same list (or briefcase you take home or desk load of paperwork), you will feel guilty for not completing it. Instead, pare down the number of items on your list. If they all *have* to be done, then you need to figure out which commitments you must eliminate to make time for those priorities.

Try to do only one activity at a time. Talking on the phone while you're writing notes may or may not be more efficient than concentrating on one task at a time, but working at a frenetic pace only adds to that feeling of being out of control. The fewer things on your to-do list and the more blank spaces in your day, the better you will feel.

If a task is really difficult or too much of a hassle, just don't do it. Too many times, you may be putting a great deal of time and effort into something that doesn't seem to be going well, with the belief that if you just try harder, you will eventually be able to do it. Some chores are just not meant to be done, and in the long run, life would be a lot simpler if you let go of those and focused on what goes smoothly. If it's not easy or requires too much maintenance, stop doing it!

It is noteworthy that "home maintenance" and "yard work and outside home maintenance" were two of the most frequent daily hassles listed by middle-aged adults during a 9-month period (Kanner, Coyne, Schaefer, & Lazarus, 1981). Research has also shown that these little inconveniences of everyday life are actually better predictors of mental and physical distress than are dramatic life changes (DeLongis, Coyne, Dakof, Folkman, & Lazarus, 1982). An unpleasant encounter, a jammed machine, being stuck in traffic, or being put on hold for long periods of time—all of these minor nuisances can be pretty stressful.

Strive as much as possible for low-maintenance living at home and at work, and review your habits on a regular basis to figure out how to simplify your life to make time for the things that you enjoy, those that are meaningful to you, and those that are essential for your overall mental health and well-being.

Keep It Simple, Stupid!

The acronym K.I.S.S. (Keep It Simple, Stupid) applies strongly to the psychotherapy profession. Working as a therapist can be one of the simplest and most hassle-free occupations, but many professionals allow it to become complicated. Anyone who has worked in an overcrowded agency or has used a temporary office knows that, essentially, the only tools you need—in addition to a box of Kleenex—are yourself, a couple of comfortable chairs, an appointment book, and folders for keeping records. If you are in private practice and have your own office, you will, of course, want to have more furniture, including a place to store files, as well as personalized stationary, business and appointment cards, a telephone, and client information and superbill forms, although these forms are optional and depend on how you like to practice. THAT'S ALL. You *don't* need a computer, a fax machine, or a secretary. You *don't* need several offices. You *don't* need to spend your precious time filling out forms or haggling with insurance clerks, and you *don't* need to hire someone to do all that for you, either. Just keep it simple! All you have to do is what you were trained for—be a therapist.

Many years ago, before computers were prevalent, I attended a luncheon where several therapists were present. One of them was boasting about a computer system he had set up so that at the end of the day, he only had to spend an hour entering his notes and recording his billing—this in addition to several hours every week sending out bills and keeping track of finances. Spending 5 to 10 hours every week on billing is efficient? All the other therapists in the room who wrote their notes and kept track of their billing by hand were incredulous. They didn't have to stay an extra hour every day to do paperwork. They simply wrote their notes by hand after their sessions, and "billing," for the most part, consisted of receiving a check from the client at the end of the hour and recording the amount: no mailing of invoices. That's all. Why make something so simple so complicated? Keep It Simple, Stupid!

Just as you don't need a computer to manage you, you don't need a fancy organizer. Get rid of yours if you have one, unless it really makes your life easier. Many years ago, I received a beautiful, large day planner for my birthday. I wanted so much to use it but realized that it was totally impractical for me. It took up too much room, and I couldn't carry it in my purse or take it everywhere with me. Sadly, I returned the gift and exchanged it for something I could use. I continued using my 6" × 4" appointment book, which is small enough that I can carry it anywhere. It also has an alphabetized telephone section where I jot down clients' numbers so that I can return their calls when I am not at the office. Although an organizer is meant to organize your life, it may actually complicate it, because (a) it is too bulky to carry around, (b) you can't make appointments on the spot if you don't have it with you, and (c) it takes up unnecessary time if you have to check your calendar or phone your secretary (if you have one) to return a call.

This system works for me. My other colleagues may have easier, less complicated systems. John uses an even smaller notebook that he always keeps in his shirt pocket. Pina has a large calendar that remains on her desk at all times. She makes appointments only when she is in her office and tells clients to call her only at those times. Sandra doesn't even own an appointment book; all scheduling is done through her secretary. Don prefers his palm pilot, which he keeps with him. Figure out which system works best for you and choose the simplest, easiest one for your needs. Just remember to *keep it simple!*

As with billing, note taking, and making appointments, look at all the other aspects of your work, and brainstorm the least complicated way to do your routine activities.

Minimize the Paperwork

Decreasing the amount of paperwork you have to deal with can simplify your life tremendously. Recordkeeping, filing, and other administrative tasks do not need to be difficult or take up much time. After all, you are only one person, and at the most you will be keeping track of 20 to 30 clients a week. How much extra time do you need for that? You don't need a system or an organizer to manage you! If you are spending a great deal of time filling out endless forms or have to hire someone to do that for you, it may be time to rethink your practices. I would like to talk about some things that have worked for others and for me in getting rid of the "clutter."

Before I went into practice for myself, I worked at an agency where a secretary handled all the billing. I didn't concern myself with details and perceived dealing with insurance companies as an awesome, mysterious, complicated task. Many new therapists feel the same way. I assure them that if they could make it through graduate school, they can probably fill out an insurance sheet. I use a small, simple invoice form that I "inherited" from another therapist. The 8" × 5" superbill has my name, address and telephone, license, and tax I.D. numbers on top. On the left are listed several office procedures, such as individual therapy, psychological testing, or consultation, with a small box next to them where I simply put an X beside the appropriate category and the amount billed. On the right are spaces to fill in the patient's name, address, insurance number, and diagnosis. There is also room for my signature at the bottom. It comes in three copies—for me, the insurance company, and the client. Because I have stopped third-party billings, I have simplified the procedure further and only have now two copies, one for me and one for clients to submit if they wish.

Some insurance companies have their own forms. Most have an adaptation of the Health Insurance Claim Form (HCFA) format. When I used to bill the insurance directly, I would fill out the entire form, except for the dates of service, xerox it, and once a month put in the dates. At the most, this task would take me a couple of hours a month. Now it takes me practically no time at all. With a few exceptions, clients pay me at the time of service, and, usually, their cashed check is the only record they need. If they wish to submit their claims to an insurance company, I give them a copy of the invoice form, warning them that a diagnosis is required for reimbursement. In that case, I fill out their name, the fee, and a diagnosis code and sign the form, letting them add the other details themselves. I usually prepare this at the beginning of the day and hand it to clients when they pay. After each session, I write down the payment on numbered arithmetic paper in their folders. My recording procedure is very simple. I have three columns: *Date, Amount,* and *Amount Paid,* under which I enter the appropriate information. I jot down notes, if needed, after an entry, such as "Will mail" or "Will pay next week." That way, if there is a blank under the "Paid" column, I know that it is not because I have forgotten to enter it. When I used to bill insurance companies directly, I had four columns instead of three: *Date, Amount, Paid (Self),* and *Paid (Insurance).* I can tell at a glance what is outstanding when I look at my records. It is simple, and you don't need a degree in accounting or a computer to figure it out. I also don't waste time mailing clients invoices at the end of every month, because they pay at the time of service. Other clinicians may have other ways to bill and record payment, but I have found this to be the easiest and least time-consuming—not to mention the nearly 100% collection rate that occurs when I use this method. Of course, all of this assumes a cash-only practice, free from managed care. Leaving managed care is the ultimate simplification if you are in private practice. I will discuss this at length in the next chapter.

Like billing procedures, writing notes about clients does not have to be a major undertaking, either. Many therapists wait until the end of the day to either dictate long notes on their sessions, which a secretary types up, or enter these on the computer themselves. Not only is this procedure inefficient and time-consuming, by the time they write their notes, sometimes days later, they don't remember important details of the session. Except for the initial meeting and a few complicated ones where detailed note-taking is required, putting a brief entry at the end of each session of all the highlights need take only 5 to 10 minutes at most. I try to do that after every hour before seeing the next client. Good record keeping is important, and the easiest way to do that is when the information is still fresh in your mind. In addition, when the notes are brief and handwritten, it is much easier to review them at the beginning of the workday before seeing clients than it is to wade through piles of paperwork. Although record keeping can be simple, it still needs to be careful, both for your protection and for the sake of your clients. Ellen Luepker provides detailed information on this topic in her book *Record Keeping in Psychotherapy and Counseling: Protecting Confidentiality and the Professional Relationship* (2002).

Minimizing paperwork will simplify your work life to a large extent. Some years ago, I spent time consulting on a research project. One of my most vivid recollections of that experience is of employees carrying stacks of folders. Everything was xeroxed in several copies, and we were constantly walking around with hunched backs, holding thick wads of paper, paper, and more paper! Aside from an aching back, I remember feeling overwhelmed just *looking* at the sheer volume of files. To find something, I had to dig through an endless bureaucracy of minutiae. Anything important got lost in large reams of pages. Endless paperwork saps energy; it did mine.

Faxes contribute to the huge mountains of correspondence, memos, and other written memorabilia that take up time and space. Faxing has become so commonplace that more and more people are using it to send or receive information, when a simple phone call will do. The same goes for e-mails. If you use e-mail, be very selective about whom you give your address to. You may wish to use it to correspond with family and friends, but do you really want to spend lots of time going through "junk" mail? If it's really important, people can call you. Similarly, if something is really necessary, they can mail it to you. E-mail and fax machines are great energy drainers and are time-consuming. Although they may be essential in some businesses, psychotherapy is not one of them!

A study of Internet users found that the more people used the Net, the more stresses and hassles they had daily (Kraut, Kiesler, Boneva, Cummings, Helgeson, & Crawford, 2002). Heavy Internet users also became more lonely and reported more depressive symptoms than did light users. Although many of the negative effects dissipated in a 3-year follow-up, the stress level remained high. Whether users feel pressures as they wade through increasing quantities of mail, with less time to spend with friends or family, or whether they feel frustrated with the complicated computer activities, the fact remains that spending a lot of time online is not necessarily good for your mental health!

Fanning and Mitchener (2001) cite a simple trick that many well-organized people use to deal with papers: Handle each piece just once to keep it from piling on your desk. Instead of sorting and resorting the same sheets and watching them stack up, deal with each one right away by doing one of the following: throw it away, file it, reply to it, delegate it, or schedule it to be completed by a later date, if it is too time-consuming to be dealt with immediately. The rewards for this are a clean desk, no constant reminders of what needs to be done, and ultimate peace of mind.

Downsize, Downsize, Downsize

Let's take the case of two hypothetical therapists I'll call Melissa and Penny. Melissa rents two offices, one on each side of town, to make her referral base larger. She has a full-time secretary and is on numerous managed-care panels. In addition to having her assistant answer some of her calls, Melissa also has voice mail and carries a pager 24 hours a day to deal with messages and emergencies. Although her secretary handles much of her paperwork, Melissa has to do the bulk of it herself, filling out diagnostic data and treatment plans for insurance companies and speaking to case managers. She receives only a reduced fee for managed-care patients. That amount is further decreased because she has to spend additional time filling out forms and requesting and justifying sessions, time that is also frequently boring at best and frustrating at worst, what with being put on hold for long periods of time and arguing with case managers to allow her to treat her clients. She usually works until 9 P.M. five nights a week, often endangering her safety when she leaves by walking alone in a dark, secluded parking lot. She spends much of each weekend trying to catch up with her paperwork.

Penny, on the other hand, goes to the office only 3 days a week and leaves promptly at 5 P.M. or earlier, if she doesn't have clients scheduled until then. Often, she goes to the movies in the afternoon with her daughter or her sister. She does not belong to any managed-care panels and maintains a cash-only practice. She does not have a secretary and doesn't own a pager. She has only a third as many clients as Melissa but has less overhead (no employees or second offices), less hassles, and more free time (no paperwork or constant paging). Penny also makes more per hour than Melissa does. Melissa gets less per case and spends more time on each one. Financially, Penny and Melissa come out about the same. The emotional cost? You do the math.

More is not necessarily better: more clients, more hours, more work. Tim Kasser, in his book *The High Price of Materialism* (2002), drawing on many years of empirical data, shows that materialistic values actually undermine people's well-being and make them feel more burdened. The desire to do "more" and have "more" goods means that they must constantly work harder and, once possessing the goods, have to continually maintain, replace, insure, and upgrade them. The irony is that rather than producing happiness, materialism creates more stress and frenzy.

Bigger is not better. In fact, when you look at models of excellence, they are usually small operations with personalized services and little or no bureaucracy. I have seen organizations get so big, they stop functioning altogether. I have watched several well-run mental health offices expand their operations, hiring more and more people, working more and more hours, which resulted in worse service to patients, until the system finally collapsed.

How many clients can you service efficiently and still give the level of care they need? How much can you expand without hurting yourself and the people you counsel? What is enough? Although the tendency is to constantly upsize and want "more," downsizing and simplifying are a wiser option. When you calculate your true hourly wage and how much it may be costing you physically and emotionally, cutting costs makes a great deal of sense.

Downsizing doesn't mean poverty, deprivation, or doing without, unless the "without" is something that you don't need and that is causing you stress to begin with. Why, for example, does Melissa have two offices? Is it really necessary for her to have a wider referral base? Is it worth the commute and the high overhead? Why, for that matter, does she need a secretary and a pager? Could she do without them? Of course!

Take a good look at your expenses and see what you can purge. As Fanning and Mitchener (2001) write, "Would you spend more carefully if every dollar you wasted took five minutes off your life expectancy?" (p. 52). Start with the obvious big items, such as house and car, and go on to the smaller ones. How many "life units" could you save if you kept your car for a few more years, moved into a smaller house, or shared an office with someone?

The large items may be easier to manage than the little ones. My good friend repeats this mantra to herself when she goes shopping: "Want versus need, want versus need." This helps her when she is tempted to buy on impulse. She recognizes—over and over—that she doesn't need that new tablecloth, that adorable pair of shoes, or the latest best-selling book. In fact, a few minutes after she leaves the store, she has forgotten about them.

Study your expenses, big and small, and figure out how many items you can reduce or eliminate. After attending a workshop on private practice sanity, I decided to apply one of the principles about downsizing. One small adjustment I made was canceling my subscriptions to some magazines. I soon discovered that (a) I did not miss them at all (in fact, it was getting to be a chore to keep up with them), and (b) I started getting free samples of magazines on a regular basis. I found this happening with other items as well. Whenever I reduced an expense, I learned that I don't miss it very much and that somehow I can get some of what I want from another source.

Reducing your need for certain items and services can be quite liberating at times. Of course, only you can determine which possessions make your life easier and which have become a burden. If you decide that you would like to simplify your life by downsizing, the books I mentioned earlier offer some concrete suggestions on cost-cutting strategies, including taking a spending break and "making do," rethinking your buying habits, getting out of debt, breaking the money habit, living within your means, and investing in the future.

Embracing the "simple path" and recognizing your true mission and priorities in your life and your work will help you and your clients in more ways than you can imagine. This sentiment has been particularly true in the wake of the terrorist attacks, when many people who were racing too fast through life found themselves drawn to the simplicity movement and wanting to spend most of their time on meaningful pursuits. In the next chapter, I will discuss one of the best ways to simplify your work life: eliminate managed care.

Self-Assessment

To make your life more maintenance-free, look at each task you undertake and ask yourself how important it is, whether it needs to get done at all, and if you can make it less time-consuming. Do the same for objects and possessions.

Which tasks do I not need to do at all?

Which tasks can be made simpler and less time-consuming?

What possessions do I have that I haven't used for years, that lead only to clutter, and that require maintenance? Which ones can I get rid of?

Which of these suggestions for low-maintenance living can I use?

_____ Reducing my work hours

_____ Scheduling my day to start an hour later

_____ Ending my day an hour earlier

_____ Giving up the "busy work"

_____ Decreasing my "to do" list

_____ Doing only one task at a time

_____ Eliminating activities that are too difficult or too much hassle

_____ (Other) ____

Am I using the simplest, least complicated way to do my routine activities?

_____ Scheduling

_____ Billing

_____ Note-taking

_____ Correspondence

_____ Paperwork

_____ (Other) ____

If not, how can I simplify those tasks?

"More" is not necessarily better. Review your responses for cost-cutting in Chapter 7.

Are there additional ways of downsizing that I have overlooked?

CHAPTER 11

Eliminate Managed Care

"The Rape of Psychotherapy"
—Ronald Fox, on managed care

If I had to make only one suggestion about changing your outer environment to become a happy therapist, it would be to say good-bye to managed care.* That is why I have put it in a chapter by itself, instead of lumping it together with other stresses to delete from your work. In addition to the time-consuming paperwork, the poor payment, and the frustration of working within the restrictions imposed by managed-care companies—I don't need to spell these out for you—managed care is toxic—toxic for you and toxic for your clients.

If you are an independent provider and feel the noxious repercussions of belonging to a panel, you are not alone. In one of the largest studies of its kind, involving thousands of licensed psychologists in both full-time and part-time practice, *four out of five* reported a negative impact of managed care on their practices (Phelps, Eisman, & Kohout, 1998). This was true for both young and older clinicians and new graduates, as well as those firmly established in their careers. The ethical dilemmas created by managed care were a significant concern for all practitioners.

Fully 67% of therapists have listed managed care as a major stressor that they have experienced (Sherman & Thelen, 1998). Working more hours for less pay is a minor part of the picture. Many clinicians feel that they have to choose between earning a living and compromising their values by sacrificing their clients' privacy and confidentiality, as well as their own standards of treatment. Again, that is only the tip of the iceberg and

---

*For readers in other countries who may not be familiar with the term, *managed care* is a system for controlling health costs by rationing health-care services to the population. To reduce costs, insurance companies manage the health care of patients by several methods, such as authorizing only a limited number of sessions, requiring a review of the patient's treatment before permitting continuation of services, setting caps on fees, allowing patients on these plans to see only providers on their panels who agree to these restrictions, and other cost-cutting strategies. For more detailed information on managed care, refer to Sanchez and Turner (2003).

doesn't even begin to address the ultimate violation, which Ronald Fox (1995) calls "The Rape of Psychotherapy" in his article of the same name.

Managed care assaults the ethical foundation of our beings as psychotherapists and humans. It debases the values expressed in the preamble of APA's first ethics code (1953), that the worth of a profession is measured by its contribution to the welfare of man. As Laura Brown (1997) so eloquently puts it, "Such values are currently in danger of extinction. The social forces that threaten to strip life; vitality; and, most important, a sense of meaning from the work of psychotherapy and to take the sinews and flesh off and leave dry bones in their place are those that urge psychologists to see the financial costs to corporations as more important than the emotional benefits, to others as well as themselves, deriving from their work" (p. 452). She further adds that managed care has intruded into those "holy places, which for psychotherapists are those places of connection between human beings who come together to witness distress and create more healing" (p. 453).

Laura Brown articulated the essence of what I was feeling about the managed-care movement. For me, the core of therapy had always been a trusting, *sacred* relationship between two people, an activity I had been engaged in for many years, one full of meaning. When managed care became the norm, I, along with other psychotherapists, tried to join as many panels as we could, as that was "the wave of the future." For the first time in years, I stopped enjoying my work. I was left with a quiet, uncomfortable feeling that something was wrong. Yes, I hated the paperwork, the intrusions, and the frustrations, but I sensed it was more than that. I was bothered by the troubling ethical dilemmas of belonging to a panel—the lack of confidentiality, the putting of profits over adequate care, and the double bind of divided loyalties, of having to choose what was best for my client versus what was best for the insurance company. Laura Brown and others put into words for me what was happening inside, and I quickly came to the realization that I could either work for my clients or for the managed-care company. I could not do both. The choice was obvious. I immediately sent out letters of resignation to every managed-care panel I was on. It was one of the most liberating things I have done as a therapist. I could not elect to continue to be a part of that system without compromising myself or those who came to me for therapy. Once again, I was able to be true to myself and my values.

Yes, managed care is toxic. It kills the very core of who you are as a therapist, and it also shortchanges your clients and their rights to privacy, confidentiality, respect, and the treatment they deserve. It is, at best, a waste of time and an unnecessary expense for you and, at worst, a violation of your clients' rights. It may also, unfortunately, be more expensive for your patients in the long run. Having a diagnosis or a "preexisting condition" can increase future insurance premiums and even make some people uninsurable in certain situations. Janet Pipal (1997) addresses this topic well and cites cases where people were denied life insurance, disability insurance, and even job clearance.

Look at it from the point of view of those who come to you for help. Although proponents of managed care tout its cost-saving benefits (for whom?), that is largely a myth (Groth-Marnat & Edkins, 1996; Miller, 1996). In addition, they neglect other factors that clients value more. In a study of consumers of mental health services (Kremer & Gesten, 2002), the main findings were that most people wanted autonomy in treatment decision making and a greater choice of therapists—clearly not possible in restrictive HMO plans. Although it is true that many consumers also expressed a desire for lower-cost therapy, "results from this study indicate that many current and potential customers of mental health services are less than pleased with changes in service delivery to realize these savings" (p. 193). Clearly, clients are not getting what they want.

Not only are clients not getting what they want, they are not getting what they deserve. "You get what you pay for" may be applicable to many patients who have these restrictive plans. Martin Seligman's (1995) exhaustive *Consumer Reports* study on the effectiveness of therapy, which found that treatment of at least 6 months provided more gains than did shorter treatment and 2 years provided the greatest gains of all, certainly calls the very brief HMO-managed health-care model into question.

You may be thinking, "I know how damaging managed care can be, but I still have to pay my bills." Like many therapists, you may feel that you have to choose between compromising yourself and your clients and earning a living. "If I resign from all managed-care networks, I won't have any clients," you might say to yourself. That may or may not be true, but if you are feeling the stress and dissonance of being part of a dysfunctional system, resign from a few panels at a time. Start out with the ones you have the most conflict with and go on to the others. You do not have to leave all of them or all of them at once.

You may be surprised to find that many clients are willing to pay out of pocket, even those who belong to HMOs. Janet Pipal (1997) disputes the belief that only a very small percentage of psychotherapy consumers are willing to consider treatment not covered by insurance. She states that she has not found this to be true in her practice, especially after she educated her clients about the ramifications of bringing a third party and a diagnosis or treatment paper trail into the therapy process. Many persons coming for therapy elect to pay out of their own pockets, particularly if there is a sliding scale. Some clinicians prefer to charge a lower fee and avoid the hassle of dealing with insurance companies, where they receive a reduced rate anyway. If you would like to do that, you can say something like, "My regular rate is _____ , but if this is a hardship case, I adjust it between _____ and _____ . You can decide where you fit within that range."

Usually, clients who pay their own way are more motivated and work harder and more efficiently than those whose treatment is covered by a third party (Pipal, 1997). Another advantage to having people pay up front out of pocket is that there is an almost 100% collection rate. It may be a myth that you have to join managed-care panels to make a living.

If you are interested in building a practice free of managed care, I would encourage you to either attend a workshop or read a book on the subject. Janet Pipal (1997) gives hundreds of strategies on ways to do that, using your skills to help people, without being dependent on third-party payers. In addition to traditional psychotherapy, she discusses other areas, including organizational consulting, mediation, educational forums, workshops, coaching, and various nonmedical approaches. You might also wish to pick up Dana Ackley's book *Breaking Free of Managed Care* (1997), or *Saying Goodbye to Managed Care: Building Your Independent Psychology Practice* (2001) by Sandra Haber, Elaine Rodino, and Iris Lipner, to learn ways to build an independent practice to benefit you and your clients.

What are the advantages for you of simplifying your life and following some of these principles? Perhaps excerpts from a letter to Janet Pipal from a therapist who did just that may inspire you. The writer hoped that her message would encourage other clinicians to eliminate managed care and its debilitating effects. She writes that in addition to increasing her earnings while decreasing her rates, having a zero balance in virtually all of her accounts, and feeling freer, feeling lighter, and living more in harmony with her values, she has found many emotional advantages to leaving managed care: "The freedom and renewed energy gained from removing myself from the ethical conundrums and the anxiety of gaining approval from those who's [sic] values and goals were antithetical to mine cannot be understated. In retrospect I don't think I myself could acknowledge the burdensomeness of the cognitive (and emotional and spiritual) dissonance I was juggling until I had gotten some distance from it. It's like finally moving away from a big dysfunctional family—with time and distance, you see how crazy-making it is!" (Pipal, 1997).

The writer of this communication goes on to report that she feels she is doing better work and is noticing that "a different sort of client is showing up . . . not necessarily higher SE status, but people who are more willing to take responsibility for themselves and work to change what is making them unhappy."

If you are enrolled in managed-care panels and feel some of the moral and emotional dilemmas of those "dysfunctional families," maybe the previous testimonial will spur you to wave good-bye to them. If you have to make only one change in your work to delete the energy drainers and make room for the things that count, resign from managed-care networks. In the next chapter, I will discuss how to eliminate other toxicities from your job by learning to set limits.

Self-Assessment

If you belong to any managed-care panels, ask yourself:

What have been some of the effects of managed care on me?

On my clients?

If I am feeling the dissonance of belonging to managed-care networks but can't afford to leave them altogether, which of these ideas can I apply in my situation?

_____ Resigning from a few panels at a time, starting with the ones I have the most conflict with

_____ Setting up a sliding scale for clients who pay out of pocket

_____ Exploring other areas where I can use my skills that don't involve third-party payers, for example, coaching, organizational consulting, and so on

What is my action plan if I decide to cut back on or break free from managed care?

CHAPTER 12

Learn To Set Limits

Run your practice instead of letting it run you.
—Sarah Nelson, psychiatrist

Saying no can be the ultimate self-care.
—Claudia Black

This chapter is about setting boundaries. It is about eliminating stresses in your life that consume time and energy. It is about saying no to all of those activities that drain you, the things you do because you "should," when you would rather be doing something else. What do you say no to? Say no to managed care and other toxicities. Say no to people who are unwilling to pay for your services. Say no to demands from organizations and colleagues. Say no to never-ending paperwork. Say no to anything you don't want to do that saps your time and energy. This leaves you time to say yes to what you want to do, those things that nourish you and feed your soul. Although many of these suggestions are more relevant for therapists in private practice, you can still utilize some of them if you are employed by an organization.

Say No by Setting Policies Up Front

It is always easier to say a big no right at the beginning so that you are not constantly in the position of having to refuse someone over and over. For example, if you have a policy that you don't work evenings or weekends, that automatically screens out clients and colleagues who expect you to. If you don't want people e-mailing you business material, it is best to let them know that right away, rather than having to spend hours every week downloading material. Here are some examples of formal or informal policies:

"My working hours are Monday through Friday from 9:00 to 5:00."

"A 24-hour cancellation notice is needed to avoid charges."

"I don't use my e-mail for business."

"I don't do hospital work."

"I don't do managed care."

"I don't bill insurance companies directly but can provide you with a superbill that you can submit to them."

"I don't treat _____ ."

"I don't do court work."

"My office is not equipped to deal with 24-hour emergency care."

"I do not have access to the type of medical care that certain conditions would require."

"I am unable to provide the level of care that you need and deserve."

These are all examples of policies that you can make for yourself and can let others know in advance to avoid problems later on. It is, of course, best to decide what your own boundaries are and to inform others about them before they have expectations of you or make demands that you will find it difficult to say no to.

Whenever possible, tell other people what your policies are immediately. With clients, this most often can be done verbally in the initial telephone contact, when responding to questions. You can also do this later on if they make demands on you that you may not wish to accept, such as deferred payments. To that, Janet Pipal says, "It is not my policy to carry my clients financially." You may also choose to put limit-setting information on your voice mail, for example, "This is Dr. _____ . My working hours are _____ . Please leave your name and number, and I'll get back to you during normal business hours." You may want to have your policy written on your appointment cards, for example, "A 24-hour cancellation notice is required to avoid payment," or on the intitial client form, "Payment is expected at time of service." Whatever policies you decide to enforce, in either your personal or your professional life, be clear in your own mind what those are and let other people know about them in advance. A clear *no* at the beginning saves many headaches later on.

Some of the clinicians I surveyed said that defining their boundaries and informing their clients about these were successful strategies they have used to deal with the stresses of being a therapist, as in the two comments that follow:

"Adopting clear boundaries re: fees, which eliminated 'exceptions.'"

"I allow myself to be very clear in what a client might be able to expect of me and where my limits are—more liberal use of 9-1-1 and explaining to clients when I would use it for them and when it's more appropriate for them to use, versus feeling that reaching me is imperative before doing anything for themselves."

Note how the word *clear* keeps coming up. Being clear up front eliminates "exceptions," late night calls, and other hassles.

Screen, Screen, Screen

Screening is setting limits in advance. The well-known saying "Marry in haste, repent at leisure" applies to the therapy process as well, and you may wish to heed it before you take on someone as a client. Screening can be done over the telephone, at the initial session, or even later, but the sooner you pay attention to those "red flags," the better off you are. Which clients do you want to eliminate? These include clients who will be unreliable and not show up; those who will not pay; those who will call you at all hours and violate your boundaries; those whose problems are beyond your area of expertise, comfort, or capabilities; and those who abuse or scare you, or both. Fortunately, most clients do not fall into any of these categories, but even one or two can cast a pall and add to your stress level.

Screening is often a two-way process. If your hours, rates, location, or other factors don't fit for someone, you discover that immediately before scheduling an appointment and thus save both of you unnecessary time. Other times, you need to have your eyes and ears open for those subtle and not-so-subtle "red flags." Some of these are easy to spot right away. A few years ago, my answering service called our home with an emergency for a "Dr. Weiss." I telephoned the man who had placed the call and asked him which Dr. Weiss he wanted to speak to, because both my husband and I are psychologists. He replied that it didn't matter. He had anxiety, and he was calling every psychologist in the phone book! I asked him how long he had been feeling anxious, and he said, "25 years"! I knew that if I didn't screen him out immediately, I would be getting "emergency" calls for the next 25 years! Several warning signs went up with that brief contact. Even though my voice mail explicity states to call the emergency number only "if you are my *client* and this is an *after-hours* emergency," this man called in the middle of the day for a condition he'd had most of his life. He apparently called every psychologist in Phoenix as well.

What other "red flags" do you look for? For me, it may have to do with either blatant or subtler boundary violations, such as when callers immediately ask you to make exceptions for them. Other alerts are when they say they have seen many other therapists and that nobody can understand them, then spend the rest of the time bad-mouthing previous therapists. I inwardly cringe, knowing that the next person to be bad-mouthed will be me. I also pay attention to my own gut reaction and to other tip-offs, such as "See what you made me do" and similar interactions. If a client tells me I'm the only one who can help her, if she says "yes but" to all my suggestions, if I'm constantly in double binds or feeling angry or frustrated, if I feel I'm in a game not of my own making, or if I sense my borders being threatened, my antennae immediately go up.

I also weed out clients whom I don't have either the expertise or the facilities to treat. I get many referrals for people with eating problems. In these cases, I question further before making an appointment. Although I am very comfortable working with binge-eating and bulimic clients, I do not have the medical backup nor do I choose to work with anorexics, who may require hospitalization and other medical care. These are only a few examples of people I try to screen out, particularly if I don't want to deal with emergency calls or hospitalizations. Your own boundaries may be different. Just know what those are in advance, and pay attention to any warning signs.

If you don't screen on the phone, you can still do it in the first session or after the second or third. If there are alerts sounding off, trust your instincts and intervene right away. To use the marriage analogy, break it off after a few dates before you tie the knot. When I sense an interaction in the initial session in which I feel that clients have a different agenda than working on their problems, what I usually do is give them a homework assignment or a task related directly to the presenting complaint and place the responsibility for completing it squarely on their shoulders.

My good friend, a psychologist, told me that she fired a couple who supposedly came for marital counseling but whose agenda was to see who could inflict the most harm on the other partner. She told them she did not wish to be a participant in what they were doing or waste her time or their money. Don't play anyone else's game or unwittingly become a part of it. Don't work with people or organizations where your gut says no, whether it impinges on your safety, your values, or your integrity. Also, don't see people you don't respect or would never associate with otherwise. It may be possible to have unconditional positive regard for most people, but not for everyone.

What about clients who frequently don't show up for appointments, cancel at the last minute, or don't pay their bills? These types are not always possible to spot immediately. Late cancellations, no shows, and unpaid bills cannot be eliminated completely, but they can be minimized. Letting clients know in advance that there is a charge for missing appointments and canceling without a 24-hour notice is a good start. Different therapists have their own ways of handling this problem. If the reason for the late cancellation is beyond one's control, such as sudden illness or a car accident, I will not require clients to pay. However, if it is within their control, for example, "I was running late" or "I have too much work," I expect payment. It depends on the situation, but usually after the first "no show" or last-minute cancellation, I will say something like "I won't charge you this time, but if it happens again, there will be a charge." I never have to mention it again, and they learn the rules quickly.

Most clients pay at the end of the session and seldom run up a tab. I have some people who come to see me who prefer to pay for several sessions in advance. Most therapists like myself, who have patients pay at the time of service, seldom have problems with collections. Most people expect to pay for psychotherapy just as they do for any other service, and unpaid bills are not an issue in most cases. I have had very few clients where this has been a problem, and in those situations, the best advice is to nip that in the bud before it gets worse. There is an old adage that says, "If a man cheats you once, shame on him. If he cheats you twice, shame on you." In other words, if you have 1 or 2 unpaid sessions, it reflects on the client. If you allow this to continue to 9 or 10, then you may want to explore some of your own attitudes about collections. Some therapists have mixed feelings about charging for helping others (Herron & Welt, 1992), and a few major ethical dilemmas for many clinicians relate to money matters (Pope & Vetter, 1992). I will explore some of these beliefs further in Chapter 21, when I discuss managing your inner world. If ambivalence about charging for providing a service you enjoy doing, for "just listening," or whatever the case may be is keeping you from having adequate collections, it is important to set and expect fair compensation (Parvin & Anderson, 1999).

Sharon came to see me for grief counseling after a stillbirth. She said she had forgotten her checkbook and would pay me at the next session. I gave her an SASE with the bill and asked her to mail it, but she didn't. She also did not pay at the second session and promised to send payment by mail. She canceled her third appointment because of illness, never sending the check. I called her, and she said she'd do that when she got paid the following week. I asked her to send me a postdated check, which I would not cash until then. She promised she would but didn't. I contacted her a few more times. Each time she said the check was on its way, but it never arrived. I realized that she wasn't going to keep her word and sent her a letter summarizing her broken promises and expressing regret that she would abuse the trust of someone who had helped her in her time of need. I ended the note by saying, "I trust you will do the right thing." A part of me had judged Sharon to be an honest person. Had I perceived her as someone who took advantage of others, I would not have wasted more time and energy by writing her. When I didn't hear from her, I wrote it off as a loss and promptly forgot about it. Six months later, I was surprised to receive a check in the mail. At first, I didn't even recognize her name on the envelope.

Having clients pay after every session ensures a good collection rate. Self-addressed, stamped envelopes and postdated checks are also good if people forget their checkbooks or do not currently have funds in their account. If, in spite of these measures, they still don't pay their bills, then at least cut your losses before the tab builds up to a large amount.

Set Boundaries between Your Home and Your Work Life

Of Janet Pipal's (1997) list of "Ten Spiritual Truths" for therapists, three have to do with boundaries. Her first spiritual truth is "Good boundaries are holy," and the second is "Phones are not holy." Another of her truths is "Good boundaries ripple through the universe." In the study of passionately committed psychotherapists mentioned earlier (Dlugos & Friedlander, 2001), the therapists in the sample took great pains to create both physical and psychological boundaries between their professional and their personal lives. They recognized that this was necessary in order to maintain their passion and to prevent burning out on the job.

If you want to avoid burnout, it is essential to draw clear lines between your home and your work life; otherwise, you'll never get a chance to recharge your batteries. Experts on avoiding burnout consistently give this advice. A key to preventing yourself from becoming emotionally and physically drained from your work is to turn off the job at home. That means no pagers, phones, e-mails, faxes, or other paperwork that intrude on your off time. If your office is located outside your home, just leave everything in a locked drawer or a file and attend to it when you return. It will still be waiting for you when you get back. If your office is in your house, lock the door when you are not "at work," and set clear boundaries between off and on times. Whatever your work hours are, be very clear about those, and make your off time your own—otherwise, you'll constantly feel stressed and frazzled. As Elaine St. James (1994) states, "My weekdays are devoted, for the most part, to my work. . . . But my evenings and weekends are my own. They have become sacred, and learning to say no to things I don't want to . . . has kept them inviolate" (p. 204). Notice how the word *sacred* comes up when describing the time away from work. Yet many people are willing to contaminate these holy moments and be "on call," even when they are on vacation. They check e-mails, voice mails, and other electronic devices that add stress to their lives, and they have their pagers on at all times. Turn off those devices when you are not at work. If you are interested in ways to separate your home and your work life, I recommend Dr. Barbara

Mackoff's little book *Leaving the Office Behind* (1986), in which she provides over 100 practical ways to turn off the job when you get home.

Wearing a pager ensures that you will never get any rest. If you have one, get rid of it immediately; or use it only for emergency calls from your children or family, not for business calls. I, for one, have never understood why therapists need pagers. Are they going to interrupt a therapy session in the middle if they get paged by another client? If someone needs to reach me, I have voice mail and an answering service for after-hours emergencies. I can count on my fingers the number of times that I have been called. If I'm on vacation, a colleague generally covers for me.

What about crises? Don't you need to be there at all times for your clients? The answer is no. Even if you wanted to, you couldn't. You can have coverage when you are away. At other times, you can be available as much as possible. I try to use the same guidelines regarding emergencies that I expect from my doctor and other service providers. I try to be very considerate of their time and call them only during business hours. If there is a true medical emergency during off-hours, I hope that they or someone covering for them will be there. Most of my clients are very respectful of the boundaries but also will call if there is a true after-hours crisis. At those times, I am grateful that I can be helpful to them. If a client abuses that privilege, I will talk to him or her about it.

Several years ago, a woman I was seeing in therapy called me on Thanksgiving because her mother (who had ignored her all of her life) had not paid attention to her on this day as well. She called me to complain about how that had ruined her Thanksgiving! It reminds me of the story of the patient who woke his therapist in the middle of the night because he couldn't sleep!

A colleague of mine shared with me that one of her clients continually called her late at night because he was anxious. She told him that she didn't have the kind of practice where she was available at all times, and if he couldn't contain his anxiety until the next morning to contact her, she would have to refer him elsewhere. The calls stopped. This approach works for most clients who call at inappropriate times. Letting them know what the limits are and enforcing boundaries keeps the late calls in check. If they are unable to stay within the boundaries, then they obviously need more than a typical outpatient practice can handle.

Try as much as possible to keep your home and your work life separate. Sandra would work all day, come home with a briefcase full of papers, and do her paperwork and return phone calls after dinner. Much of the time, she would be too fatigued to do much of anything and would feel guilty for not doing the office work. She felt like a school child who had homework all the time. Sandra taught, in addition to being a therapist, and her students and colleagues called her at home to discuss a thesis, a research article, or any other work-related project. She also had piles of e-mails waiting for her. Sandra dragged around, exhausted, especially toward the end of the semester, feeling drained, burned out, and depleted. When she became involved in a relationship, she could see how much her work was intruding on her personal life, and she made up her mind to set strict barriers between them. First of all, she decided which days she would be at the office and used her voice mail to convey that information to callers. When she was at work, she did all of her paperwork there and left at a specified time. What she didn't complete remained in a locked drawer, instead of in her briefcase. When she came home, she relaxed, leaving the e-mails, phone calls, and paperwork to deal with when she went to her office. When colleagues or students called about something, she either let the answering machine pick up their messages or told them nicely that she was too tired to think about work and would talk to them the next day. Sandra was surprised how easy that was for her to do and how rejuvenated she felt once she set clear lines between her professional and her personal life.

A balanced life is important. If there are no boundaries between work and play, then you will constantly be working. "Time out" every evening keeps you refreshed, rested, and available to your clients.

Delegate, Delegate, Delegate

Lorna, a psychiatrist, came to see me because she needed some balance in her life. She was newly married, and the demands of her job were interfering with her fully enjoying her personal time. The truth of the matter was that she loved her job, but there was too much of it, with the result that she felt drained, fatigued, and burned out. She worked in an inpatient facility, and every time she stepped outside her door, someone wanted something from her. Lorna was a very conscientious individual and liked to do a good job. There were just too many demands on her. Most days she went without lunch and at times didn't even have a few minutes to go to the bathroom! She rarely was able to leave work at 5:00 P.M.

Lorna decided that she needed to set some limits, not only within the job, but between her work and her home life as well. She took a good look at her responsibilities and recognized that she clearly had to eliminate some of those. The hospital was short-staffed, and even though she was able to get rid of some duties, she still had a lot on her plate. Lorna first set up some boundaries at work. Because she was "attacked" by people every time she stepped outside, she stayed in her office and left a "Do Not Disturb" sign on the door when she was doing paperwork. She also made plans to take a lunch break every day—outside the hospital!

Although Lorna was less frazzled after setting these limits, she still felt that she didn't have "enough hands" to do it all. Aha! Maybe some other hands could help. Lorna was in charge of a fairly large department that had several residents whom she supervised. She recognized that she actually had quite a few other hands out there that she could give some of her work to. Lorna knew that she had a tendency to micromanage and want to do everything herself. She was able to parcel out more and more tasks to others, and even though they were not always done as perfectly as she would have liked, they were "good enough." This freed her up from many of her responsibilities and the myth that she was the only one who could do them. In fact, she discovered that the more she did, the less others did! Now she gave them a chance to expand their responsibilities. Parceling work out to others can improve your personal and your professional lives tremendously. It enables you to accomplish more in less time and do the jobs you are most suited for and that are high on your priority list (Bolton, Bolton, & Adams, 2002).

"Delegate, delegate, delegate." An alternate of this is "Refer, refer, refer." When people ask your help for something and you find it difficult to say no, give them the name of someone else who can do the same job. This will benefit both you and the one making the request. You will feel good for having helped that individual, and the person will also get the information he or she needs. Joanie frequently gets invitations to speak at conferences. Although she is flattered and would also like to help the various organizations seeking her expertise, she doesn't have the time. When she is asked, she says, "I am afraid I won't be able to do that, but I can provide you with some names of others who also specialize in that area." The person making the request is usually pleased to get the referral, and Joanie doesn't feel guilty for saying no!

Learn Nice Ways To Say No

"I know all about saying no. I teach my clients every day how to do that—but when it comes to my doing it, it's not easy," said Len, a social worker. If you're like Len, you probably know all the right reasons for saying no. Yet at times the words just won't come out of your mouth when someone asks you for something. If that is the case, give yourself a break and, instead of blurting yes and regretting it later, buy yourself time. Say, "Let me think about that," "Let me check my schedule," "Let me ask my husband or wife," or anything else that keeps you from responding immediately to the request. In fact, make it a point to always do that unless you know 100% whether you wish to accept or refuse. This gives you time to think and decide, "Do I really want to do it?"

What guidelines can you use in deciding whether to say yes or no? One that I find helpful is: Is this a "want" or a "should"? If it's something I feel I should do but don't want to, I usually say no. Another guideline that is often useful is that if it's not easy, don't do it! I don't mean easy in the sense that it is not challenging; I mean if you dread every minute of it, if it takes up a lot of senseless energy, or if it seems like a great deal of trouble, it's probably not worth doing!

Ben was invited to give a lecture to a class on his area of specialization. He said yes right away, because he usually enjoyed talking to students. A few weeks later, he was told to submit a resume and a summary of his speech. He did that and was then asked to send a picture of himself. He was surprised by the request but mailed one in anyway. A few days later, he received a call that the photo was not the correct size or color and that he needed to send in one with the specified dimensions. That meant he would have to go and have his picture taken. At that point, Ben decided that this was way too much trouble just to give a talk and said no to the whole idea. If it's not easy, just don't do it!

If it's not simple and you're already in the middle of it, get out just as Ben did. Resign from any committees or organizations whose meetings you dread. If, like Ben, you said yes to something because you anticipated that it might be fun and it turns out to be complicated, leave! If you thought you had signed on for something (talking to students) and then it got to be something else (having your picture taken), get out!

When you say yes, whenever possible, spell out your level of commitment up front. That way, there will be fewer misunderstandings later on. Lynette joined a group to provide volunteer services for needy people. A few days later, the leader of the organization called her, asking for her e-mail address so that the leader could send her "interesting" articles. Lynette said she didn't use her e-mail for business and wasn't interested in reading articles, only in doing counseling. The chairwoman kept insisting, and although Lynette became uncomfortable, she stuck to her guns and didn't give out her e-mail address. However, the pushy interaction was a harbinger of what was to come. A few days later, the woman called again and informed Lynette that she had to attend a social function with other members of the group that week. At this juncture, Lynette clearly specified what her amount of involvement with the organization was going to be: no e-mails, no "extracurricular" socializing, only a few hours every month providing therapy services. Lynette stated what her limits were and decided that if the leader kept "testing the limits," she would resign from the organization.

What are some nice ways of saying no besides "Let me think about it"? Here are some other ways:

"My schedule won't allow it."

"I just can't fit it in right now."

"It just won't work for me."

"I'm so glad you asked, but I just can't make it."

"I am unable to provide you with the level of care you need and deserve."

Or, as one of my friends who had a busy job, three youngsters, and lots of extra responsibilities, used to say, "Not this year!"

I have found that what makes it easier to refuse a request is telling myself, "If I say no, it will feel awkward for a minute or two but if I say yes, it will mean (5 hours of work, a dreadful evening, lots of aggravation, a $100 contribution, or whatever else I'm saying no to)."

Say Yes to What You Want

When you say no to what you don't want, you are saying yes to the things you want: good clients, good hours, good friends, meaningful work. You are saying yes to the life you want to create.

Whose life is it, anyway?

Self-Assessment

What are some policies that I can set up front to minimize problems later on?

What types of clients do I want to screen for? What are some "red flags" for me?

Do I have clear boundaries between my home and my work life? If not, what are some ways to keep my home and my work life separate?

What tasks can I parcel out or refer to others?

Are there any "should" or "difficult" energy-draining activities that I want to say no to?

If yes, what's keeping me from doing that?

Part III

Tips for Managing Your Inner Environment

CHAPTER 13

Clinician, Know Thyself

Question: What is the therapist's most valuable instrument?
Answer (and no one misses this one): The therapist's own self.
—Irvin Yalom, *The Gift of Therapy*

In Part II, I discussed how to change your outer environment and make it work for you. This section is about managing your internal world—your thoughts, your feelings, your body, *yourself*—so that you are a happy and effective therapist. To learn to navigate your inner world, the first step is to know yourself and keep yourself optimally functioning at all times. In psychotherapy, probably more than in any other profession, you are the instrument, and you need to keep that tool sharp, to tune it regularly and take care of it, not only to avoid your own burnout, but so that you can do your craft and be effective for your clients. Because so much of being a therapist depends on "being there" emotionally and being attuned to your own feelings and experiences, it is essential that you get a clear reading when you are conducting therapy, rather than one colored by fatigue, distractions, and distortions.

As Dr. Lorna Smith Benjamin (2001) states, "therapists ought to be as careful about their state of alertness as, for example, airline pilots. It is important to keep the caseload sane, to be well rested, and of course, to keep one's proper emotional balance in relation to patients and their struggles" (p. 26).

What does knowing yourself mean? It means recognizing your physical and emotional limits. It means paying attention to when you feel burned out. It means listening to your gut and learning to trust it, in and outside the therapy room. It means trying as much as possible to keep your instrument—yourself—clean and clear, so that you can know how much of what you are getting comes from you and how much comes from the client. It means sensing what fraction of what you are experiencing consists of your own issues and what belongs to the person you are treating. It means checking over and over again how much of what is happening is inside you and how much is inside your client's head. It means listening to your reactions, using them as diagnostic tools, and making sure they are not colored by your distortions—not an easy task.

My good friend, who had been up for several nights with a new grandchild and who in addition had been battling a cold, told me that she had seen a woman in therapy the week before, and for the first time in her life she couldn't remember anything that had happened in the session only a few days ago. She wondered how much of that was her own fatigue and how much had to do with the client. This is the kind of thing you need to check on regularly, as a therapist—what proportion of your reaction comes from you and what proportion your patient contributes.

One of the most useful tips I ever received from a therapy supervisor was, "You know the client is acting when you find yourself reacting." If I start to get annoyed, bored, scared, or protective or to experience any number of other feelings, I try to figure out what part of my reaction comes from what the client is doing to elicit these emotions in me and what part is my "stuff." To do that, of course, I need to know myself and to keep my "instrument" as accurate as possible, so that my diagnostic impressions are not skewed by instrument errors. In the next few chapters, I will discuss ways to keep your apparatus clean and to recognize when you need a tune-up.

CHAPTER 14

Take Time To Sharpen the Saw

Sometimes the best thing you can do for yourself is to take a nap.

—Anonymous

Stephen Covey, in his best-selling book *The 7 Habits of Highly Effective People* (1989), uses sharpening the saw as a metaphor for self-renewal. A man is working furiously to saw down a tree and is exhausted by the labor and how long it is taking him. "Why don't you take a break for a few minutes and sharpen the saw?" you ask him. "It would make it go faster." "I don't have time," he says. "I'm too busy sawing!" Take time to sharpen the saw: physically, emotionally, socially, mentally, and spiritually. To be an effective—and happy—therapist, you need to keep your instrument, yourself, sharp at all times. There is a direct link between well-being and personal effectiveness, and both therapists and their consumers suffer when therapists do not take the time to take care of themselves (Kearney, 1990; O'Connor, 2001).

Sleep, Exercise, and Do All Those Good Things

One day as I was trying to get into my car, I found that the key kept getting stuck. I noticed that I was also having difficulty starting the car, and from time to time, the key would lock in the ignition. I kept ignoring this because I didn't want to take the car to a mechanic, who, I was certain, would suggest big repairs. However, one morning, when it took me at least 5 minutes to get the car started, I decided I couldn't disregard the problem any longer. Dreading having to get a new engine and fearing that the vehicle would require a major overhaul, I finally went to a repair shop. The car mechanic took one look at my car key and showed me how it had gotten bent! I was looking for complex solutions instead of a simple one. I was seeking complicated, deep-seated, external causes for the problem instead of the obvious one—my key was out of shape! Similarly, if you are feeling tired, frazzled, unmotivated, or lethargic, something as basic as a nap or a good night's rest may be the answer—like the key, you may simply be "out of shape." If you find yourself unable to "start the car" and get yourself going, look for simple answers within yourself, rather than outside you. Make sure that your "key," your "saw," your working "instrument"—yourself—is intact.

I recall hearing at a workshop that the best predictor of happiness is adequate rest. I tell that to my clients and find it to be true for me as well. If I'm tired, I feel irritable and cranky, and an easy task seems overwhelming. If I'm feeling rested, I'm able to take most things in stride. Sleep is so important that I could write a whole book on it. Fortunately, I don't have to. Dr. James Maas has already done that. His book *Power Sleep* (1998) provides the scientific data on the major role sleep plays on your physical, emotional, and mental functioning, and you must learn to value it as much as you value exercise and proper nutrition. According to sleep experts, if you want to be in a good mood, energetic as well as mentally sharp, you need to spend at least *one third of your life sleeping!* Sleep restores, rejuvenates, and energizes you. As Dr. Maas writes, "The third of your life that you should spend sleeping has profound effects on the other two thirds of your life, in terms of alertness, energy, mood, body weight, perception, memory, thinking, reaction time, productivity, performance skills, creativity, safety and good health" (pp. 6–7). If you feel that sleeping is a waste of time, ask yourself how much your safety, health, and general well-being are worth.

Just how much sleep do you need? Maas states that researchers are finding evidence that we may require as much as *10 hours of sleep* every night. Although most individuals can function okay on 8 hours, 10 hours is best for optimal performance. Most people are significantly sleep-deprived and have become accustomed to it. As Maas states, "Many of us have been sleepy for such a long time that we don't know what it's like to feel wide awake" (p. 61). The consequences of sleep deprivation can be disastrous at worst, such as when you fall asleep at the wheel, or very unpleasant, at best. You feel drowsy, irritable, bored, sluggish, foggy, and generally unhappy.

Are you getting enough sleep? Maas suggests a simple test for sleep deprivation. Lie down in a quiet, dark, and cool bedroom and try to go to sleep as quickly as you can. If you don't fall asleep within 20 minutes, then you are getting adequate rest. If you fall asleep within 5 minutes, you are not getting enough sleep. Other ways to tell if you are sleep-deprived are if you need an alarm clock to wake up, if it's a struggle to get out of bed in the mornings, if you sleep later on weekends, if you have trouble concentrating or remembering, or if you fall asleep watching TV, at a boring lecture, or after a heavy meal or a low dose of alcohol.

Dr. Maas's "golden rules of sleep," in addition to having an adequate amount of shut-eye nightly, are to establish a regular sleep schedule and to make up for lost sleep so as not to build up a deficit.

Helen, a young woman in her 20s and a bundle of energy, looked positively exhausted as she talked to me. Normally a conscientious and dependable individual with an excellent memory, she had forgotten and missed some important appointments. She was tearful and could barely say a word without crying. She couldn't understand why she was so depressed, frazzled, and disoriented and kept searching for deep-seated psychological causes for her mental state. Just one look at her, and it was obvious that she was too fatigued to even think straight. I urged her to just go home and take a nap. She had several commitments scheduled well into the evening, but she agreed that she was unable to concentrate anyhow and that her presence at those was not essential. She canceled her meetings, went home, pulled down the drapes, took the phone off the hook, and had one of the most luxurious naps she had ever experienced. When she woke up, she was alert and clear-headed—and the world looked bright again! Sometimes the best thing you can do for yourself is to take a nap!

Sleep, rest, proper diet, exercise, vacations—basic self-care—these are the ABCs of sharpening the saw. Coster and Schwebel (1997), in their article on well-functioning in professional psychologists, report that one psychologist said we should write the following words on our office wall: "Rest, relaxation, physical exercise, avocations, vacations." They recommend that these avenues to personal well-being be established very early, preferably in graduate school. This is often easier said than done, particularly when the demands of postgraduate training are so great.

Most of the clinicians I surveyed listed physical self-care as crucial to being a happy and effective therapist. Below are some typical responses:

"Sleep. Eat well. Relax. Take great vacations."

"Make sure you take care of yourself all the way."

"Take care of your body through diet and exercise."

"Take time for relaxation and for lunch, and take at least two consecutive weeks for vacation."

"Take care of yourself physically—jacuzzi and massage."

In addition to a good night's sleep, good nutrition is important for proper functioning (Faelton, 1996). Although many therapists give this advice to their clients, they often fail to follow it themselves. Frequently, they skip breakfast, lunch, or both, running on empty, going nonstop for

6, 8, or 10 hours straight. If you are skipping meals because your day is too fast-paced, now is the time to reverse the cycle. A simple breakfast need not take more than a few minutes and prevents sluggishness during the day. And lunch? Try to go out for lunch at least once a week. The break, in and of itself, is good. When you don't eat out, bring something from home and take the time to eat it.

Exercise is also one of the elements of good, basic self-care. Even 5 or 10 minutes a day can make a difference in your overall well-being. Exercise, in addition to its many physical benefits, has a physiological effect on your moods, increasing endorphin levels and giving you a psychological boost (Byrne & Byrne, 1993; Leith, 1998). Exercise need not involve big chunks of time or money. It does not have to mean taking precious hours of your day to go to the gym after work. A brief walk, a daily swim, a few minutes on the treadmill, or whatever it is that gets your body moving will make you feel good!

Vacations are also essential to self-care. Even a brief getaway can help you come to work fresh, rested, and ready to go. Longer holidays are important as well. Strive for at least 2 continuous weeks of vacation every year, in addition to mini-vacations. Three or 4 weeks are even better!

Know Your Physical and Emotional Limits

Although a general guideline is to have 7 to 8 hours of sleep, three meals, daily exercise, and frequent vacations, your own individual needs may vary. Each person has different bodily requirements. Recognize what yours are and honor them. Know your physical limits, your energy level, and your personal stamina. How much sleep do you need? How much rest? How many client hours a day or a week can you handle without getting fatigued? How often do you need to go away to recharge your batteries? Learn to monitor yourself and find a rhythm that works for you. If you are a racehorse, you may need a faster tempo than if you like to take things slowly. Find your optimal pace, somewhere between rusting out and burning out.

Recognize your emotional constraints as well. Try to limit the number of clients you take on who drain you or leave you feeling traumatized. If there are certain types of problems that you find too close to home or that leave you feeling vulnerable, it is better to recognize that right away, rather than to continue listening to heartbreaking stories that you cannot distance yourself from. Many therapists, for example, will not work with abused children because they cannot deal with the pain of it. One way of taking care of yourself is understanding what your emotional limits are and not exceeding them. Remember, the providers most likely to suffer from compassion fatigue are those who are caring and empathetic (Figley, 1995).

Observe yourself and watch for cues when you are going beyond your physical and emotional boundaries. One of the most effective research-based strategies and a top-ranked contributor to optimal therapist functioning is that of self-monitoring and awareness (Coster & Schwebel, 1997; Norcross, 2000). Therapists need to be cognizant of the early warning signs of distress, when they need to ask themselves if the workload is too heavy or the time for leisure or sleep is too little. Sometimes, feedback from friends and spouses can also be helpful. If your intimates tell you that you're looking tired or haggard, listen! Norcross (2000) calls this process of attending to and monitoring your internal states *self-liberation,* which he defines as the acknowledgment, the commitment, and the burden of replenishing yourself, professionally and personally.

Balance, Balance, Balance

A balanced life has been described as one with equal space devoted to work, relationships, and self, or "I" time, those activities that sharpen the saw, that nourish and renew you, to make you more effective in the other two areas. If love and work define you and make life meaningful, then attentiveness to self helps you give your best to these. What is "I" time? It is quality time—for yourself. It's spending at least 30 minutes a day on yourself—take a bubble bath, go for a walk in the park, read the paper, sit in the sun . . . do whatever it is that rejuvenates you. Although a balanced existence may not always be possible, with "I" time and relationships frequently getting shortchanged, you can at least try hard to prevent your life from getting too lopsided and allowing one area—usually, work—to dominate, neglecting yourself or your friends and family in the process. That is also the main conclusion in a study on physician burnout: Balance is necessary for healthy functioning, and professional impairment is more likely to result when too much emphasis is placed in one sphere, to the detriment of others (Coombs & Fawzy, 1986).

What is balance? It is learning to do things in moderation and not giving 100% to all that you do. It is attempting a little of something, rather than letting it consume you. Some things don't need to be done perfectly, and some don't have to be done at all. It is pacing yourself so that you are not depleted. Balance is the key, not only in how many clients you see or in your professional activities but also in the rhythm of your daily routine. In other words, don't do marathons!

Christina Maslach (1982) puts it well: "If all the knowledge and advice about how to beat burnout could be summed up in one word, that word would be *balance.* Balance between giving and getting, balance between stress and calm, balance between work and home—these stand in clear contrast to the overload, understaffing, overcommitment, and other imbalances of burnout" (p. 147).

Incorporate Relaxation, Meditation, or Other Forms of Spirituality into Your Life

Learn to sharpen the saw spiritually as well. There are many different ways to rejuvenate your soul. Relaxation, meditation, self-hypnosis, yoga, prayer, being in nature, listening to music—whatever it is that lets you get away from the daily, mundane tasks and allows you to see the "big picture," do it. Whatever it is that allows you to develop a sense of peace and gives you perspective, make room for it so that you don't get bogged down in the details. Whatever it is that helps you see the meaning in your life and your work, make the time for it.

Research has demonstrated the many physical and mental benefits of the regular use of relaxation, meditation, or both in your life. A review of the studies on different types of meditation, including the relaxation response, biofeedback, mindfulness meditation, and yoga, shows significant links between these types of practices and reduced blood pressure, lower cholesterol, increased relaxation patterns in the brain, and reduction in stress and anxiety—to name only a few of the beneficial effects (Seeman, Dubin, & Seeman, 2003). There is also considerable empirical support for the linkages between spirituality and optimum mental and physical health (Miller & Thoresen, 2003; Powell, Shahabi, & Thoresen, 2003). These findings are hardly surprising and underscore the importance of sharpening the saw spiritually.

Being with nature can be a form of spiritual experience, and we have already seen some of the restorative effects of "green" settings in Chapter 5. You can combine exercise with being in natural environments. Walking, running, jogging, and swimming are all activities that you can do in beautiful surroundings, and they can be as restorative for the body as for the spirit. Are there any environments that you are drawn to? Are there any places that give you a sense of serenity and well-being? Whether it's the beach, the mountains, the park, or even your own backyard, leave the noise and chaos behind and give yourself up to the peace, quiet, and beauty of nature. Take time to meditate, enjoy the scenery, and be in harmony with the outdoors.

In this chapter, I have focused primarily on physical ways of sharpening the saw. In the following chapters, I will discuss ways of renewing yourself emotionally, socially, mentally, and spiritually. The next chapter is about learning to recognize and avoid the emotional depletion of burnout. Later chapters will address other methods of self-care, including personal psychotherapy, supervision, networking, and colleagues.

Self-Assessment

Rate yourself on how well you are "sharpening the saw." Take a look at each of the following forms of self-renewal:

_____ Sleep

_____ Proper nutrition

_____ Exercise

_____ Staying within my physical and emotional limits

_____ Balance between work, relationships, and "I" time

_____ Incorporating relaxation, meditation, and other forms of spirituality into my life

In which areas am I taking care of myself as well as I can?

Which areas can I improve on?

How?

CHAPTER 15

Learn To Recognize and Avoid Burnout

If all the knowledge and advice about how to beat burnout could be summarized in one word, that word would be balance.
—Christina Maslach, *Burnout: The Cost of Caring*

Preventing burnout is the flip side of "sharpening the saw." It is not just taking care of yourself to become more "sharp" and effective but also to avoid the incapacitating effects of burnout. Learning to recognize and prevent burnout is essential to all practicing therapists, and I feel that every graduate program in the mental health professions should have a course in its curriculum devoted to that topic. Unfortunately, very few do, and many clinicians learn about burnout the hard way, by experiencing its disastrous results and the unfortunate consequences for them and their clients.

What Is Burnout?

Burnout is more than being sluggish and tired. In its extreme form, it is experiencing such depletion that you cannot take on one more task. It is being so emotionally exhausted that you start resenting your clients and fantasizing about leaving your job. It is feeling so detached from others that you start avoiding them. It is being numb but continuing to go through the motions. It is getting overwhelmed and frazzled and not knowing how to break the cycle. It is having absolutely no energy and feeling depressed.

In fact, the symptoms of burnout and depression are so similar that if you are burned out, you may think that you are experiencing a major depression. Yet although the two may feel the same, their causes and treatment are different. Depression is frequently brought on by loss and characterized by grief, but burnout is due to excessive stress and fatigue. Both are marked by an erosion of energy. Depression can result from burnout exhaustion if the burnout cycle is allowed to continue.

To understand burnout, let us look at some of its definitions. Freudenberger and North (1985) define it as "a wearing down and wearing out of energy. It is an exhaustion born of excessive demands which may be self-imposed or externally imposed by families, jobs, friends, lovers, value systems, or society, which deplete one's energy, coping mechanisms, and internal resources. It is a feeling state which is accompanied by an overload of stress, and which eventually impacts on one's motivation, attitudes and behavior" (pp. 9–10). Please re-read this definition carefully. You will notice certain words that keep cropping up when people talk about burnout: *wearing down, wearing out, exhaustion, excessive demands, depletion of energy, overload of stress.* This cumulative overload can at times result in very observable and tragic behavior changes.

Jerry Edelwich and Archie Brodsky (1980) define burnout as a progressive loss of idealism, energy, and purpose experienced by people *in the helping professions as a result of their work.* Although burnout can occur in any field, individuals in service careers are more vulnerable. What happens to therapists who work intensively with others, day after day, listening to their emotional problems? Ideally, practitioners should be able to do so without losing their concern for their patients. Unfortunately, that is not always the case. Christina Maslach (1976), who has studied the dynamics of burnout and coined the term, found that a large number of helpers cope with stress by a form of distancing that hurts not only them but their clients as well. Many mental health workers begin to feel cynical and negative about the people they treat, often viewing them with contempt and even believing that they deserve the problems they have. They "detach" from their patients, by either seeing them as less than human, giving them derogatory labels, or using scientific jargon ("the coronary in Room 3," "the obsessive-compulsive," etc.). They also distance themselves physically by standing away, avoiding eye contact, or spending less time with them. Often, there is avoidance of clients altogether. Unfortunately, this detachment can filter into their home lives as well, with resulting estrangement from family and friends. Many clinicians feel they are "bad people" for having these feelings and do not realize that other therapists share these feelings as well when they are burned out.

The effects of burnout can be devastating for you and your clients unless you take steps to prevent them. Although burnout does not necessarily have to result in therapist impairment, therapists are most apt to engage in unethical behavior or make decisions that hurt their clients when they are extremely burned out (Stadler, 1990). Burnout does not always happen, but certain work conditions are more likely to produce it. Maslach states that burnout is inevitable when a professional must care for too many people, resulting in higher emotional overload. She compares a burned-out worker to a wire that just had too much electricity and it emotionally disconnects. *It is not the number of work hours that brings on the burnout but the number of hours in direct patient contact* (Maslach, 1982). If you are your own boss, you have control over how many people you see. If you are in a setting where the demand is excessive, you may be a prime candidate for burnout.

Remember That Burnout Starts with the Compulsion To Prove

I have permanently marked a page in Freudenberger and North's (1985) book on burnout that I show to people who are burned out. Because they don't have time to read and don't need to do "one more thing," I briefly go over with them the chart on page 196 that outlines the burnout symptom cycle, instead of asking them to read the whole book. The authors have a circular illustration that shows at a glance how burnout can develop gradually and mushroom into an epidemic without early prevention. Burnout begins with the compulsion to prove. This is where you may say to yourself, "I'm not just going to do a good job. I'll do the *best* job ever. I'll be a *supertherapist*. I'll give it my *all*." It is a compulsion because there is a driven quality to it, a pressure and an urgency, a preoccupation with the job to the exclusion of other interests. This is followed by an intensity, where the overenthusiasm, the "fire" takes over, leading to subtle deprivations of those things that renew or refresh you. This is when you skip eating breakfast, reading the paper, getting a haircut, or meeting friends for lunch just because you don't have the time. I talked about the importance of "I" time in the previous chapter: This quality time with yourself is even more essential for preventing burnout. Those little rituals are necessary for recharging your batteries or, as a colleague of mine likes to put it, "stocking up the well" or "filling up the gas tank." Otherwise, you're running on empty.

If you don't intervene early on in the burnout cycle, the symptoms are likely to get much worse. "Oh, it's not that bad," you might say; or, "I don't need to read the paper daily" (or whatever little thing you are doing without). In fact, denial is one of the characteristics of burnout (Freudenberger, 1986; Kottler, 1993). If you continue stripping away small luxuries and negate the importance of these subtle deprivations, burnout can result in disengagement, emptiness, depression, and, in its extreme form, total burnout exhaustion. If you are starting to eliminate some "extras" from your daily routine, reinstate them back immediately! As one female therapist told me half in jest, "Now I can go and shave my legs again!"

How can you tell if you are beginning to feel burned out? If you find yourself getting cranky and irritable or if you're snapping at people, that's probably a tip-off that your "fuse is short." If you are eliminating more and more enjoyable activities because you don't have time for them, then you need to go back to your basic routine. If you observe yourself getting impatient with loved ones or even wanting to avoid them altogether, that can also be an indication that your batteries need recharging. If you are getting overinvested in a client's welfare or a project and are taking more and more responsibility for it, at the expense of other commitments, that can be a cue to back off. If you are experiencing feelings of anger or contempt toward your patients and cringe at the thought of another therapy session, then it is time to "restock your well."

Learn the Four Burnout Stages and How To Intervene at Each Step

Edelwich and Brodsky (1980) discuss the different phases of disillusionment for people in the helping professions. I have found those to be so useful that I have summarized them in outline form and regularly review them with the therapists I supervise or counsel. The authors dilineate four stages of burnout and interventions for each one. Ironically, burnout starts with *enthusiasm.* I have heard it stated that the people who are most likely to get burned out are those who are most on fire in the first place. This is where you go into a job giving it your all—and then some! You don't just give 100% but 150% or 200%, depleting your resources before you even start. This is the initial "honeymoon" period of inflated hopes, expanded energy, and overidentification with clients. This stage is most common in beginning therapists. They are going to be "supertherapists" and do what nobody else has done. If they care enough, if they do enough, they will see change. They often have very high and often unrealistic expectations, both of themselves and of their clients, and they end up feeling disappointed when all their hard labor goes down the drain. They "work" much harder than their clients and do just "one more thing." Soon they find their energies depleted, and they start getting resentful. Or they may overidentify with their patients and take the patients' problems home with them. Or they may start to feel inadequate because they don't see any progress in the people they are treating. The outcome can be particularly devastating if they have clients who make excessive demands on them and then berate them for not being better therapists! I have supervised a couple of students who were ready to leave the field altogether after such interactions.

In their extensive studies on the professional development of psychologists, which included 160 practitioner interviews over a 6-year period, Thomas Skovholt and Michael Ronnestad (2001) have found that less experienced therapists do not have adequate information about the change process and may believe that they can be responsible for overnight changes. Consequently, they may give it their "all," believing that if they work hard enough, dramatic changes will follow.

Not only beginning counselors start a job with fervor. In a study of clinical psychologists, the sample as a whole scored higher on "compulsive caregiving" than on other patterns of relating (Leiper & Casares, 2000). Although enthusiasm and a positive attitude are good things to have, it is *overenthusiasm* that is the killer. Overenthusiasm is when you are consumed with the work, when you are living, eating, and breathing it. It is when all of your time and energy go into it, so that you wear out your resources very quickly. To prevent burnout, one of the first things to do is not to give 100% all at once. Do things in moderation. Know your limits and pace yourself. Don't use up everything you have right away—you have limited reserves. This first stage of *enthusiasm*—or *overenthusiasm*—is the *intensity* that Freudenberger and North talk about.

At this initial stage of the burnout cycle, you need to be very careful about conserving your energy and pacing yourself so as not to get depleted. Note again that burnout starts with the compulsion to prove, and if that is the force that is driving your intensity, work on it! I will elaborate on this further in a later chapter when I discuss getting out of the overresponsibility trap. When you stop needing to prove and can learn to feel comfortable being responsible only for your actions and not for those of your clients, when you allow them to do at least 90% of the work, then you have a very strong chance of avoiding the deleterious effects of burnout.

The best time for intervention is in the enthusiasm stage—before the damage is done. The antidote for enthusiasm is *realism,* having realistic expectations instead of idealistic ones. Rather than trying to drastically alter your clients' behavior, attempt to make a few mini-dents. Focus on the successes and not on the failures and on the process instead of on the outcome, and don't look for big changes right away. Therapists with many years of experience frequently have a long-term time perspective and see progress in little actions (Skovholt & Ronnestad, 2001). It is also important not to assume too much of the blame for lack of movement or to interpret results self-referentially. Remind yourself that you did not cause your patients' symptoms.

Try as much as possible to prevent burnout in the initial states by monitoring the intensity of your workload and setting realistic expectations. This may help you avoid the second stage of disillusionment—that of *stagnation.* During this period, you are still doing the job, but it is no longer so thrilling or is no longer a substitute for other things in life. The emphasis now is on meeting your personal needs, and issues of money and career development become more prominent. The "high" of the first phase is gone. The thrill is no longer there, and you may feel as if you are in a rut. Just as realism is the remedy for enthusiasm, *movement* is the cure for stagnation, through both job-related and off-the-job interventions. Some ways of getting action on the job may be further education, in the form of either formal training or workshops. Some of the suggestions at the beginning of the book for diversifying and creating a more stimulating work environment can help you overcome the normal plateauing of doing the same task over and over again. Making adjustments on the job, such as getting supervision or joining new groups, may also be useful in giving you new and fresh perspectives. Off-the-job interventions are those that enlarge your "outside life," such as hobbies, travel, reading, exercise, and family and friends. Many ideas in the initial chapters on creating the life you want are relevant here.

The third stage of disillusionment is that of *frustration.* It is at this juncture that emotional, physical, or behavioral problems can occur. Some job settings, particularly bureaucracies, can contribute to your feeling frustrated. If you start to feel powerless and wonder what's the point of helping people who don't respond, or you ask what's the use of doing anything when the system defeats your efforts, you are probably in the third phase of burnout. If you start questioning your effectiveness as a therapist or whether the job is even worth doing, then it is time to intervene. This stage is not all bad. Although you may go along indefinitely and complacently in a state of stagnation, it is the energy of discontent that creates the possibility for change. If you are unhappy and frustrated enough, this may force you to take the actions necessary to change your life, whether this involves making adjustments at work, switching jobs, going into private practice, or leaving the field altogether. The antidote for frustration is *satisfaction,* and the very seeds of the malaise will provide the impetus to make meaningful changes.

The last stage in the burnout cycle is that of *apathy,* which is the typical defense against frustration. It happens when you feel chronically thwarted on the job, yet need it to survive. At this time, you may only be putting in your hours and giving the minimum. This, unfortunately, is common for some long-term employees, who are only dragging their bodies to work until retirement. Just as in the previous stage, both off- and on-the-job adjustments are possible, and you will need to make a strong effort to convert the apathy into *involvement.* The power beneath the inertia can be a strong force that you can put to good use. Can it be done? Yes. I have watched people who functioned as therapists for several decades, sometimes even in "burnout" environments and crazy-making systems. Yes, many of them were simply putting in their time until they could collect their pensions. But in the interval, they continued to approach their job with enthusiasm and their clients with respect and caring. How? First of all, they had a very active life outside of work and took care of themselves physically and emotionally. They had hobbies, friends, and interests apart from the job and didn't put all their eggs into that one basket. Second, they found a great deal of meaning in what they were doing and were able to look beyond the inefficiencies of the system and the chronic conditions of their clients and see the value of their work. They also had a strong network of friends and colleagues whom they shared their frustrations with. I will talk about some of these themes in later chapters.

If you are experiencing burnout, can you reverse the cycle? Of course! Lisa, the therapist whose story I described in the first chapter, was relieved to recognize her symptoms as burnout—which she successfully overcame after she made a few modifications—and not as a major depression or a personality flaw. She described her change as a "paradigm shift." She told me, "I learned to think of what I need to do to please me, instead of what I need to do to meet everyone's needs and expectations." Sounds simple, right? That's what you tell your clients every day, and yet, at times, you may find it difficult to make this shift in your thinking and behavior for yourself. Just as Lisa learned to do it, regularly ask yourself, "What do I need to do to take care of myself right now?"

I'd like to stress that burnout is not a one-time occurrence. It is not a problem that you can take care of, once and for all. Just like brushing your teeth or exercising, you need to monitor yourself on a daily basis to keep its debilitating effects from progressing to unmanageable levels.

Self-Assessment

The following is a checklist of a few common behaviors associated with burnout.

Am I currently experiencing any of these symptoms?

_____ Being cranky and irritable

_____ Eliminating more enjoyable activities in my life because I don't have time for them

_____ Engaging in "subtle" deprivations

_____ Avoiding friends or family

_____ Feeling resentful of the time I spend on others

_____ Feeling relieved when clients cancel

_____ Feeling pessimistic about my clients

_____ Daydreaming more than usual

_____ Feeling bored or apathetic about my work

_____ Becoming increasingly cynical

_____ "Medicating" myself with food, alcohol, or pills

_____ Feeling exhausted much of the time

_____ Feeling detached from clients, colleagues, and friends

_____ Distancing myself from others

_____ Feeling overwhelmed and frazzled

_____ Becoming overly invested in a client's welfare or a project, to the exclusion of other commitments

_____ Feeling anger or contempt toward many of my clients

_____ Just putting in my hours

_____ Starting to question my effectiveness as a therapist

_____ (Other) ____

____

____

If I am showing any signs of burnout, at which of these four stages do I need to intervene? How?

_____ Enthusiasm (versus realism)

_____ Stagnation (versus involvement)

_____ Frustration (versus satisfaction)

_____ Apathy (versus involvement)

CHAPTER 16

Listen to Your Body's Signals

> *Make a tally of the signals you've been receiving around any given issue—through dreams, fantasies, cravings and ambitions, persistent symptoms, the fears and resistances that have been preoccupying you lately, what books are on your nightstand, what notes to yourself are tucked on the refrigerator door. Then do the mathematics. What, if anything, do these all add up to?*
>
> —Gregg Levoy, *Callings*

In the last chapter, I talked about learning to recognize burnout in yourself and using your body's cues to become aware of and reverse the burnout cycle. In this chapter, I will discuss further how to listen to your body and use it to educate you on a daily basis. The body speaks, and, over the years, I have begun to heed its voice, to pay attention to my actions, my dreams and intuition, those valuable sources of knowledge that guide me daily. The longer I live, the more I have come to marvel at and trust the information that I can gain from attending to those sources within me, what is popularly referred to as "right brain" springs of knowledge. I have learned to rely more and more on those resources and to respect them, combining them with analytical, "left brain" thinking for best results. Although objective data are very important—you have undoubtedly spent years and years in school, learning to respect the scientific method—educating yourself about and learning to trust your own subjective, internal wisdom is just as necessary. Your body is speaking to you daily, and you can utilize its guidance in your everyday life—inside and outside the office.

How Does Your Body Speak?

Your body is constantly talking to you. It speaks to you through your intuition and hunches, when you "sense" something is wrong but can't quite put your finger on it. It speaks through your actions, when you find yourself suddenly cleaning your closets, for example. It speaks through your nighttime dreams, as well as through your daytime fantasies. It speaks through images that come to you when you are relaxing or talking to a client. It speaks through the sensations you feel when you are engaged in a task or even thinking about it, whether these be of restlessness, lightheadedness, or heaviness. It speaks through your health, when you feel achy or out of sorts. It speaks through your energy level, how fatigued or alert you are when doing something. It speaks through your emotions, when you laugh for no good reason. It speaks through the knot in your stomach when you are in the middle of a conversation. It speaks through your gestures, when you find yourself instinctively backing off or coming closer. It speaks through your memory—what you forget and what you remember—and your memories, which ones you keep coming back to.

Why should you pay attention to what your body is saying? Here are a few of the reasons: because it is likely the most accurate indicator of how you are feeling and what you need to be doing, because it may be one of the best sources of self-knowledge, because you can use it as a guide in your daily decision making, and because it is a part of you. Martha Beck, in her book *Finding Your Own North Star* (2001), says that you have your "North Star," your own built-in compass within your body, that steers you in the right direction. When you learn to pay attention to your internal navigational guide, you can connect to your essential self. When you tune out your body's signals, you may be tuning out important information. As Gregg Levoy says in his book *Callings* (1997), "If our only approach to the body's deep cries is to clamp our hands over our ears, we have dismissed the dreams of the body" (p. 92).

Jenna, a young therapist, had an uneasy feeling about a woman she was seeing in therapy. She couldn't account for the strong sense she had that her client was going to harm herself. She called her supervisor, who listened to all the objective facts about the patient's situation and saw no urgency in the matter. Jenna couldn't get rid of the uncomfortable premonition, however. She just knew something was amiss. She consulted with her colleagues, who also reassured her. The client had denied any suicidal ideation, and there was nothing in her background that would make her a suicide risk. Still, Jenna couldn't shake off the sensation that something was wrong, in spite of others' assessments of the situation. The next morning, the woman tried to kill herself. This experience, although painful for Jenna, helped her learn to listen to her own gut reactions and to rely on them. Although she didn't have objective data to support her feelings, she started to pay more and more attention to her internal cues and find ways to tap into them.

Jenna was similar to many other junior therapists, in that she relied on outside knowledge to guide her, discounting her own internal signals. In the studies mentioned earlier on practitioner development (Skovholt

& Ronnestad, 2001), it was found that senior clinicians discard many of the external crutches and rely more and more on their own expertise. New therapists, on the other hand, have little confidence in their own ways of knowing, frequently believing that the truth comes from other, more knowledgeable sources. Although openness to feedback is very important, do not hush your inner voice.

In Chapter 13, I discussed the importance of knowing yourself and how crucial it is for you as a therapist to keep your "instrument"—yourself—clean. In this chapter, I will elaborate further on tuning in to this knowledge through your body's signals—combining it with analytical judgment—to guide you, both inside and outside the therapy room.

Listen to Your Body's Sensations

Whether you are approaching a task, a client, or a friend—or even thinking about them—notice whether you are moving forward or instinctively backing away. Pay attention to whether your muscles are tensing up or whether you feel relaxed. Do you have an open or a closed posture? These are, of course, obvious nonverbal cues that you can use daily to evaluate your reactions to people or activities.

"I was swimming," said Ben, "and suddenly, I started thinking about a very unpleasant task I had to perform. I then noticed that my strokes were getting slower and slower, and I was feeling heavier and heavier the more I thought about the task." Like Ben, you may wish to use your energy level as an indicator of your reaction. Do you feel heavy when you are talking to someone? Do certain people drain you? As you attend to these internal signals, you can use them as cues as to what you are experiencing. What activities increase your stamina? Which ones make you feel light? Start engaging in those that invigorate you and get rid of those that deplete you.

Also note how fast time goes by when you are doing something. Does it flow or drag? In fact, "flow" describes how you feel when you are engaged in those activities where the hours just seem to fly, as if you are in an altered state of consciousness (Csikszentmihalyi, 1991). If your body is in sync with your actions, the time will zoom by very fast. (Think of some things you do where the hours speed by, and do more of those!) If the minutes seem like hours, ask yourself what your body is saying to you and what you need to do with that information.

Listen to your emotions. What kinds of sensations do you have when you think about or engage in a particular task? What do you experience as you are talking to a certain client? Do you feel warm, loving, impatient, resentful, fearful, or wary? If your "instrument" is clean and those feelings don't reflect your own inner problems, you can use the emotions the client is evoking in you to guide you in your work with him or her.

Sometimes your body speaks so strongly, you cannot ignore its message. "I just could not make myself get out of bed," said Sandra, a therapist who worked in a very dysfunctional environment. "It's as though my body had a mind of its own." Sandra had been dissatisfied with her job for a long time but continued to trudge on. Finally, her body did the talking for her. She simply was unable to move.

As Sandra's was, your health may be one of the strongest body signals to tune into. Many years ago, when an environment I was working at became very stressful and led to a mass exodus, several of us developed physical problems for which we had to have surgery and then left. We jokingly referred to those as our "farewell" operations, but I have no doubt that stress played a part in them. As Gregg Levoy states so eloquently, "Like a child trying to get attention, a symptom will get louder and louder over time, the signal coming across with ever-increasing voltage and violence the longer you ignore it. Health, it seems, is largely the art of listening" (p. 94).

Listen to Your Body's Actions

Prior to my having "farewell surgery," I was driving to work, a route I had taken for 10 years, and kept missing the turn to my workplace. The first time this occurred, I attributed it to inattention. This continued to happen, and each time I drove farther and farther away from my job. One day, when I traveled several miles out of the way, I knew that I had to pay attention to my actions. "I don't want to go there," my body was telling me. Of course, my movements were no coincidence. For years I had driven down that same road without "forgetting" to turn. Why now? Some years later, when I was going to a meeting at a place where I didn't want to be, I "missed" the exit again! If you find yourself regularly forgetting something, ask yourself what it is you don't want to do.

Frequently, your actions may precede conscious thought. Many people report that they suddenly get an urge to clean out their closets or throw out old projects, as though unconsciously anticipating change and making room for the new. "I didn't know that I was ready to leave what I was doing, at least on a conscious level," said Sally, "but I just found myself getting rid of old stuff and making room for something else. It's as though a part of me was preparing for the move without my realizing it."

If you catch yourself, as Sally did, cleaning up clutter, remodeling, getting a new hairstyle, having an urge to do something you have never done before, or engaging in any number of unexplained outward behaviors, these may reflect some internal changes that may not automatically be clear to you. Your body usually "knows" something before it consciously registers in your brain.

Listen to Your Unconscious

Your unconscious, your right brain, your sixth sense, or whatever you want to call it, can be a very important guide for you, and you can learn to tap into it regularly and trust its intelligence. How can you access this rich source of self-knowledge?

Dreams are probably one of the best ways to tune in to this nightly well of wisdom. More than any other venue, I have found dreams beneficial in answering the question, "How am I doing? What is going on inside me?" The dreams are helpful both personally and professionally, and I have learned to use them to guide me in my actions. A dream about my desk becoming cottony and moldy, for example, alerts me that I am feeling stale at work and serves as the impetus for starting a new project. A dream about a high-powered attorney as an awkward adolescent helps me recognize the vulnerability underneath his bravado. Your dream is like a trusted friend, an internal adviser who lives within you, who tells you how you are feeling and where you need to be going.

A therapist reported this dream to me, which helped her see a problem more clearly and become unstuck in her work with a married couple. Every Monday at 5:00 P.M., she would see the two of them together. She viewed the husband as psychotic and empathized with his wife. One night she had a dream that it was Monday at 5 in the afternoon, there was a huge storm, and her secretary announced, "Norman and Norma Bates are here!" Norman Bates is the name of the psychotic in the movie *Psycho.* By dreaming about Norma Bates, the therapist's unconscious recognized that the wife was psychotic as well, something that her conscious mind had not registered. The dream helped guide her in her treatment of this duo.

I could go on and on about the value of dreams and have, in fact, written two books on the subject (Weiss, 1992, 1999). In these books I discuss the many uses of dreams, as well as provide a step-by-step guide on how to understand them and use them, both professionally and personally. I also review the research findings on the uses of dreams (Weiss, 1992, pp. 18–36). Research conducted so far on dreams has demonstrated a physiological basis for dreaming and has established that everyone dreams with nightly regularity. In spite of the difficulties associated with conducting dream experiments, studies suggest that there is a continuity between dreaming and waking phenomena and that dreams reflect waking concerns. The research also shows that dreams are influenced by waking conditions and are not just random, meaningless activity. In addition, studies show that most individuals require a certain amount of dreaming and that dream deprivation can result in some psychological disturbances.

Many studies have supported the view that dreams have an adaptive function as well. Controlled experiments have shown the value of dreams in involving patients in their therapy and preventing dropouts. Dreams also act as a valuable source of knowledge in everyday life, helping you see situations more clearly, allowing you to become aware of your vulnerabilities, as well as pointing out your strengths. They let you tap into your creativity, work through emotions, make decisions, rehearse future situations, and solve problems. I call them your own internal "wise man."

However, dreams are not the only way to delve into your right brain. The symbols you get in your nightly voyages come through other channels as well. Relaxation, self-hypnosis, meditation, and other forms of altered consciousness are also ways of listening to your body's voice and what it is communicating to you. As you allow your mind to relax, let the images and the sensations surface, and get in touch with what they are trying to tell you. Pay attention to that free-floating wisdom that you can conjure up whenever you need it, and listen to what your unconscious is saying.

We know that creativity generally involves several stages (Samuels & Samuels, 1992). Although the first phase is consciously thinking about a problem, a period of laying it aside and allowing it to ferment is usually needed to come up with the "Aha!" experience, the time that an answer comes when you are no longer actively contemplating the issue. "I get most of my ideas in the shower," a client told me. So do many people—or while driving or engaging in some mindless task where they relinquish the matter for awhile. This stage of letting go is very important, and dreaming, meditation, and other types of relaxation provide the necessary altered state to get unstuck and for the solutions to take hold.

If dreaming is the road to the unconscious, writing and keeping a journal are secondary routes (Greenspan, 1999; Progoff, 1992). Julia Cameron, author of *The Artist's Way* (1992), coaches people on how to get in touch with their creativity. She touts the "morning pages"—three pages of longhand writing, extremely stream-of-consciousness—as the primary tool of creative recovery. She recommends making a daily commitment to fill up three sheets of paper. Like meditation and other activities, writing helps unblock conscious restraints and allows imaginative solutions to come forth. Whether you choose to write in your journal on a daily basis or only when you want to get in touch with your inner life, putting words to paper is often an excellent way to listen to what your unconscious is saying to you, not to mention the many therapeutic and health benefits associated with journal writing (Francis & Pennebaker, 1992; Pennebaker, 1993; Pennebaker, Colder, & Sharp, 1990).

Poetry is one form of writing that is particularly effective for accessing your inner voice because it is playful and has no real rules. In fact, some people believe that poems reflect the same unconscious process found in dreams and have used poetry to facilitate self-awareness (Edgar, 1978). Whereas lyrics about a particular subject may sometimes pop up spontaneously, you can free up your mind by writing a poem about that issue. Just allow the words and rhymes to come up. You may be pleasantly surprised by what you hear. I know someone who thinks in verse. Give her any topic, and within minutes, she will have composed a rhythmic masterpiece about it. Even if you don't possess her remarkable gift, when you decide to put your thoughts into rhyme and don't care how nonsensical they sound—nobody is going to read them but you—some precious gems from the unconscious may arise. Just listen to what phrases appear unbidden. Sometimes the words may not even be your own. You may hear a quotation, a refrain from a popular ballad, or a familiar tune. What songs do you hear in your head? Pay attention to the lyrics: They may provide strong clues to your internal state. Music and poetry have both been found to be effective tools to free up memories and get in touch with unconscious processes and have been widely used in the therapeutic process (LeLieuvre, 1998; Lerner, 1978).

Collaging is another right brain activity that provides an entrance into the unconscious. Get a stack of magazines and tear out photos, images, phrases, or whatever else appeals to you. You do not need any forethought or planning with this task. Later on, glue what you have cut out on a large sheet of paper, in any arrangement you wish. Whether you do a themed collage (e.g., "what I hope to accomplish next year") or not, you will find this form of self-expression another way of listening to that other voice within you, which often speaks in pictures and talks directly to your gut. I heard of a woman who makes a photomontage every New Year of what she wishes to have happen in her life the coming year. She swears that simply by looking at this display, all her desires get accomplished. What she is saying, of course, is that even though she is not consciously working on her goals, her unconscious mind is responding to those images and helping her in their pursuit. A picture is worth a thousand words.

However you choose to tap into your inner life—whether through dreams, meditation, journal writing, collage, or a combination of those—learn to listen to what your unconscious is saying to you and dip into that unlimited well of knowledge for guidance and clarity.

Listen to Your Intuition

Several years ago, I was at a bookstore in Oberlin, Ohio, waiting in line to pay for some purchases, when a book just "tugged" at me. I picked it up and started reading it. After a few pages, I couldn't put it down. I bought it and buried myself in it on the airplane, all the way back to Phoenix. It was based on the extraordinary experiences and coincidences of the writer while pregnant with her child. Halfway through, I learned that the author, Dr. Martha Beck, lived in Phoenix, Arizona. When I arrived home and looked at the newspaper, I saw not only that she resided in my hometown but that she was going to do a lecture and a book signing on another publication that week! I attended her talk and went up to her afterward, telling her about my experience. She remarked that this was no mere accident.

Synchronicity is a term for these curious coincidences that seem to happen when you are open to your intuitions and sensations. Partway through writing this chapter that mentioned Martha Beck's work on heeding your bodily signals, I had to interrupt what I was doing to go to a meeting. As I was driving to the site, I was thinking about the remainder of the chapter and what I would put down about intuition and synchronicity. I turned on the car radio, and who should be talking about following your North Star and paying attention to your physical sensations but—you guessed it—Dr. Martha Beck!

As if to underscore the importance of extraordinary coincidences and to provide me with further "material," two people told me about their amazing experiences the very next day. A man who had lost his son and had transformed his grief into a life goal of rebuilding an inner-city church unexpectedly received a $6,000 check on the third anniversary of his son's death to help with the project! A woman who had a dream about some winning lottery numbers berated herself for not acting on this information after the winning ticket was announced with those numbers. She went to a store to console herself, and next door, she saw several individuals handing out free drinks. The occasion? They had just won the lottery!

How do you explain these synchronistic events? Julia Cameron (1992), in her book on unblocking creativity, claims that as you listen to your inner voice and pursue your creative intuitions, you begin encountering helpful coincidences to reinforce this path. Incidentally, the bereaved father whose church had received a $6,000 donation, 3 years to the day his son died, told me that on that same evening, he was watching Joseph Campbell, the anthropologist, on television, reporting that people get more and more of these helping occurrences when they begin working on their life mission!

Synchronicity is, of course, also a result of focused attention. When you are looking for something, your unconscious is constantly scanning. Because I needed examples of synchronistic happenings, I was watching for those and zeroing in when they took place. Even though I was not actively searching for anecdotes for the chapter, my unconscious was engaged full time to provide me with what I needed. Whenever I'm working on a book, I have learned to trust my intuition and to have faith that if I leave myself open, the "material" will come, and if I put pen to paper, the thoughts will flow, and the words will materialize. As has been said, when the student is ready, the teacher will come.

Synchronicity is one of the manifestations of listening to your inner voice. As Martha Beck (2001) says, when you are doing what you love, events happen that seem like gifts, encouraging you along the way. When you ignore that voice, everything seems to go wrong. What is intuition? It is that gut sensation that cautions you that something is wrong, as it did Jenna, the young therapist, whose supervisor and colleagues assured her otherwise. It is the feeling that "This just feels right. Don't ask me how I know." It is heeding and acting on your inner urgings because you just "know."

Dr. Christine Page (2001), a physician who has written and lectured extensively on intuition, lists several ways of enhancing yours, some of which I already touched on in this chapter: dreams, meditation, and the arts. Other avenues are through the media or through other people. For example, often you may hear on the radio or on television a subject being discussed that brings to the surface something you are actively thinking about, just as had happened to me when I turned on my car radio while "scanning" for synchronistic events or to the bereaved dad who was watching TV and listening to Joseph Campbell affirm the importance of embarking on your life's mission.

Martha Beck (2001) suggests going to a bookstore and seeing which publications you are automatically drawn to, which speak to you and tug at you, just as hers did when I was standing in line at the bookstore in Ohio. It may be a newspaper or a magazine article that just leaps at you and provides you with the words you need to hear. Or it may be another person who says something and drops a thought into your mind that releases an inner knowing. Or it may be anything that catches your eye that has always been there but suddenly resonates with you. Note synchronistic experiences when they happen, and trust that if you act on your inner voice, you will have more and more of these helpful coincidences.

Learn to go with the flow of the signals that your body sends you. Understand your own body's unique language and act on its messages. Pay attention to your physical sensations, notice your actions, listen to your unconscious, and respect your intuition. Tune into your body's cues. They are your own built-in feedback system, letting you know when you're on or off track. Heed that voice and start trusting it. In the next chapter, I will discuss another way of gaining self-knowledge: personal psychotherapy.

Self-Assessment

Listen closely to the many ways your body is speaking to you—through your physical sensations, your actions, your health, your unconscious, and your dreams.

What are my own unique internal signals that tell me when I'm on or off track?

How is my body speaking to me right now?

What is it saying?

Which of these ways of tapping into my inner life do I want to make more use of?

_____ Dreams

_____ Meditation

_____ Journal writing

_____ Writing poetry

_____ Collaging

_____ Paying attention to synchronistic events

_____ (Other) ____

Choose at least one of these venues, preferably one you haven't used before or haven't paid attention to in a long time, and listen to your body's signals. Afterward, ask yourself what you have learned.

What have I learned?

CHAPTER 17

Get Some Personal Therapy

It is only the way the cards have been dealt that I am helping instead of being helped.

—Anonymous

I have these words, which I saw on a sign during a trip to Canada, framed on my desk, serving as a constant reminder of the value of therapy in my own life and to treat my clients the way I would like to be treated if I were coming for help. I am apparently not the only practitioner who believes that having therapy oneself is crucial to conducting it. In a large national survey on therapist attitudes and practices, fully 80% of presenting psychotherapists had undergone personal therapy and felt that personal analysis was an essential prerequisite for competent clinical practice (Prochaska & Norcross, 1983). Some feel that seeing a psychotherapist should be a mandated requirement in graduate training and cite literature that this view is overwhelmingly supported by administrators of programs in professional psychology (Gilroy, Carroll, & Murra, 2002). Not only does psychotherapy provide a priceless training experience, it also helps therapists achieve a greater degree of emotional stability and mental health. Psychotherapy helps you know yourself and, in turn, benefits your client. Your own analysis is a worthwhile way to learn about your inner workings and keeps your main "instrument"—you—sharp. In this chapter, I will discuss further the importance of counseling for your own well-functioning and for that of people who come to you with their problems.

Get Therapy for Personal Reasons

When I was a graduate student many years ago, some very major life changes were taking place with the students in my program. A large number got married during that time; an equally large number became divorced or made other significant moves. Over the years, as I have taught and supervised graduate students, I have noticed these same trends as well. Graduate school is a time of adjustments. Many of these shifts coincide with life-cycle events that occur on becoming an adult;

others come from the unique characteristics of the training environment. At any rate, this is a time of major transitions and the corresponding stressors that go with them, such as changes in finances, work, and living conditions, as well as feelings of constantly being overwhelmed and in competition with others.

Another source of tension for those training to practice psychotherapy is the undefined, ambiguous nature of clinical skills and the difficulty in performing them. How do you *do* psychotherapy? Many students walk around feeling discouraged, inadequate, and frustrated at not being able to master the task. In addition, learning to think psychologically may result in continual self-scrutiny and self-improvements, with consequent marital discord, as people make major adjustments in their lives. The presence of a high level of stress and pervasive anxiety in beginning practitioners is consistently supported by the research (Cherniss, 1995; Pearlman & MacIan, 1995; Skovholt & Ronnestad, 1995).

This period of outer and inner changes is, at the very least, stressful and confusing. Guy (1987), who has written extensively on the personal lives of therapists, cites studies showing that nearly 82% of first-year graduate students reported periods of severe anxiety, fully half had long bouts of depression lasting at least 3 days, and nearly a third had intense sleep problems. Unfortunately, it appears that anxiety and depression are the norm in beginning graduate students. To add to the distress, many of them are afraid to share these concerns with either faculty, who will be evaluating them, or fellow trainees, with whom they are in competition.

Stresses are not limited to graduate students and junior therapists. In previous chapters I outlined many of the unique problems, ranging from managed care to suicidal patients, associated with being a clinician. I also mentioned the troubling statistics, with three out of four therapists having experienced major distress over the last 3 years and more than 60% having suffered a clinically significant depression at some point in their lives (Epstein, 1997). Several recent studies only confirm these grim findings (Gilroy, Carroll, & Murra, 2001), particularly for women, who outnumber men with a ratio of 3:2 (Gilroy, Carroll, & Murra, 2002). These numbers alone are enough to encourage you to go into personal therapy.

Fortunately, many therapists do go for therapy to deal with their stresses. In a large-scale survey of psychotherapy use among clinical psychology graduate students (Holzman, Searight, & Hughes, 1996), of those who responded, 75% indicated that they had seen a therapist at some point in their lives. Although they commonly mentioned personal and professional concerns for seeking treatment, a large number got help for clinical problems that are seen in the general population, such as depression or marital or family conflicts. A disturbing finding is that nearly 25% said they had been or were depressed during graduate training. It is not just graduate students who seek therapy for their problems. Over two-thirds of practitioners receiving counseling did so to work through personal conflicts (Prochaska & Norcross, 1983).

Even if you are not experiencing any symptoms, it is a good idea to undergo psychotherapy for personal growth. A client refers to his therapy sessions as his regular "tune-up." He comes in every once in a while to make sure that everything is operating as it should. Whether you need a major overhaul or a simple adjustment, personal psychotherapy is where you will find it. The psychologists who were rated as passionately committed by their colleagues (Dlugas & Friedlander, 2001) had a hunger for feedback and supervision, and several sought psychotherapy to face interpersonal barriers and make certain their "instrument" was in working order.

In Ronnestad and Skovholt's (2001) study of senior psychotherapists, the results pointed to the need for students and practitioners to continually process and reflect upon the ways that childhood experiences affect professional functioning. Senior therapists, averaging 74 years in age, said that even in later professional years, the early years continued to exert an influence on them, and that to develop optimally, clinicians need to continually reflect on the effect of these childhood experiences. Personal therapy certainly provides a vehicle for doing that.

In my own survey of mental health professionals, many cited going into therapy as one of the pieces of advice they'd give to beginning therapists. This statement is typical of their comments: "Be prepared to undergo individual and group psychotherapy for at least a year to gain insight into your own personality and issues, as well as to sensitize yourself to the experience your clients will have."

Get Therapy for Professional Reasons

Not surprisingly, distress and professional impairment among clinicians can negatively affect their clients. Clinicians may not be able to use their skills effectively because they are not functioning at optimal level, and their work as therapists suffers (Sherman & Thelen, 1998). As Janet Coster and Milton Schwebel (1997) remind us, "We can do great service to ourselves by accepting the fact that all practitioners are vulnerable to stress and that at some point in our careers we may be on the way to being impaired" (p. 12). The impairment can impact your clients, manifesting itself in the inability to focus or in more serious ethical and boundary violations. Although this is neither a comforting thought nor something to look forward to, it is one occurrence that is easily preventable and may be the impetus to enter therapy. If you don't do it for yourself, do it for the sake of your clients. The research shows that therapists bring their own style of relating and early childhood experiences into their work, often recreating them (Jackson & Nuttall, 2001; Leiper & Casares, 2000). For that reason, an understanding of your own inner workings can be very useful in your practice, so that you are not bringing your own filters into the therapy room.

In a study examining the impact of personal therapy on clinicians' ability to work with clients, it was found that being in therapy can exert a positive influence on the practice of therapy in a number of ways (Macran, Stiles, & Smith, 1999). Through their own therapy, mental health professionals had a better understanding about themselves, about their clients, and about the process of therapy. They learned about the importance of the therapist's influence by having a role model and, consequently, experienced the need to better care for themselves and set boundaries. They also had more respect for their clients, learning to trust them and not rescue them prematurely. In addition, therapists were better able to distinguish between their own feelings and those of their clients, to work at a deeper level, and to judge the pace of therapy. This certainly suggests that being in therapy yourself can significantly improve your effectiveness in how you practice.

Another reason to see a counselor yourself is to know your product. If your profession is "doing" therapy, you need to know firsthand what that entails, what it means to be a consumer. Although many psychotherapists practice therapy full time, there is no degree in "psychotherapy." You major in social work, psychology, psychiatry, or other disciplines, and much of the time in preparation for conducting therapy is spent in didactic work in the classroom or through readings. Furthermore, many clinicians seldom get to see psychotherapy performed by experienced clinicians because therapy, by its very mature, is a private activity. Consulting a therapist provides the beginning mental health professional with a chance to observe another practitioner in action. Roughly a third of psychotherapists seeking treatment do so partly for training purposes, to get the experiential learning, to see what it feels like to sit in the client's chair (Prochaska & Norcross, 1983).

It is not surprising that the most important factor for therapists in their theoretical orientation was the influence of their own personal therapist and his or her particular framework (Guy, 1987). (One's assigned clinical supervisor was ranked as least important!) These findings, of course, make sense. It is what you experience *personally* that most affects you. You learn how to do psychotherapy by being psychotherapized, just as you learn to parent by being parented. It is not what you read and learn about proper therapy and proper parenting that impacts you as much as *experiencing* it. You learn what works and what doesn't work, what to do and what not to do. It is the empathy of having been there and knowing what it is like to be sitting in the patient's seat. Yalom (2002) sums it up: "To my mind, personal psychotherapy is, by far, the most important part of therapy training" (p. 40). I couldn't agree more!

Being a psychotherapist is different from being an accountant, a plumber, or a gardener. It is not just a line of work, a profession, but is also a way of life. Because so much of your tools are your own internal workings, psychotherapy is almost a necessity in becoming familiar with those and with the product—the service you are dispensing.

If therapy makes you a better—not to say, happier—therapist, it is unfortunate that some clinicians don't seek it for fear that they will be judged emotionally unstable or inadequate. Distressed clinicians, in particular, are reluctant to do so, despite the dangers of practicing when they are not at their best (O'Connor, 2001). The embarrassment of admitting serious problems, as well as the fear of the consequences, often gets in the way of going for help (Barnett & Hillard, 2001). There are often logistic concerns as well, in trying to find a therapist whom they don't already know personally or professionally. Even when they decide to seek help, there may be limited resources available. And, of course, there is the ingrained attitude that psychotherapists should be the prototypes of mental health! Although many practitioners would not hesitate to sign up for workshops to improve their clinical skills, some are wary of seeking the most direct route. In one study, a third of practitioners surveyed stated that they would not see a therapist, many viewing it as a sign of weakness (Deutsch, 1985).

Most clinicians who sought therapy stated that it had a positive impact on their work with people who came to them for help (Gilroy, Carroll, & Murra, 2001). As a result of their personal experience, they described enhanced empathy for their clients, more patience when progress was slow, and an appreciation for how difficult it often is to make changes, as well as more faith and trust in the process of psychotherapy itself.

In a book on the personal and professional reflections of therapists, *How Therapists Change* (Goldfried, 2001), psychotherapists of varying orientations list therapy as a major influence in their personal growth and in their work with clients. Lynne Jacobs (2001), a gestalt-analytical therapist, articulates what this experience has been for her: "I moved from a vision of myself as having certain experiences that were fundamentally impossible to share with others to a vision of myself that holds all of my experiences as potentially shareable. . . . Now my work with my own patients began to reflect the experiences I was having in my analysis. I listened closely to their vision of themselves, and I watched closely for signs that my listening failed to meet them, even in small ways. The effect on my patients was dramatic. Almost to a one, over the course of the next several months, my patients spoke of how much safer they felt to bring their most vulnerable sense of themselves into the dialogue with me. They were speaking of things they had not been able to verbalize previously" (p. 284). Here is how another psychotherapist (Mahoney, 2001) put it: "I learned the central importance of the therapeutic relationship, and I began to relax some of my needs to understand everything that was taking place in my life and my clients' lives" (p. 194).

It is often hard to differentiate the effects that psychotherapy can have on your personal life from those it has on your professional life, but seeing a counselor enhances both. Although many people would never consider learning to drive a car without getting behind the steering wheel, many therapists—and training programs—do just that.

In addition to the numerous personal and career benefits of seeking therapy, there are also many nonspecific effects, beyond those already discussed. Lawrence Perlman (2001) lists the numerous "serendipitous" gains from therapy beyond their intended effects, ranging from inadvertent role-modeling, learning to adhere to a routine, or simple placebo effects. These incidental benefits frequently generalize to other aspects of one's life, so that family and friends can benefit from these serendipitous perks.

Does Therapy Work?

If you have to ask that question, it is probably time to leave the field! Even a colleague who eventually did just that said that one of the most successful tools or strategies she used to deal with the demands of her work was "getting out of the profession and seeking therapy until I could find another job." Sometimes you may need therapy to learn that being a therapist is not for you! Martin Seligman (1994, 1995) cites the evidence for therapy effectiveness. However, if you haven't experienced it yourself, do so now by all means!

Even if you have been in therapy and are no longer seeing a therapist, you can continue to reap the benefits by having "booster" sessions by yourself. Alvin Mahrer (2000), in his advice to therapists on how to replenish themselves, suggests having experiential sessions on, for, and by yourself. In these sessions, he reserves the hour, goes into his soundproof office, reclines in a big comfortable chair, and, using a combination of meditative techniques and dreamwork, goes through a therapy session, much as he would with a client. As he says, "It seems sensible that if therapists truly have faith in their professional work, they would use these methods on and for themselves in their personal lives" (p. 229). This may not work for everyone, but if you are not currently in therapy and feel a need for a tune-up, scheduling a psychotherapy session with yourself may be a good start.

Self-Assessment

What might be (or might have been) some of the personal or professional benefits for me of undergoing psychotherapy?

_____ Developing the strength to cope with stresses inherent in the profession, other stresses, or both

_____ Gaining insight into my behavior

_____ Achieving personal growth

_____ Working through issues that may be interfering with my life or my work

_____ Experiencing what it's like to be a client

_____ Learning about the process of therapy

_____ Observing another therapist work

_____ Learning to accept feedback

_____ Making myself a more effective therapist

_____ "Serendipitous," unintended benefits

_____ (Other) ____

____

____

If I haven't already done so, what has been keeping me from going into therapy?

CHAPTER 18

Talk to Your Colleagues

If you do not have a close, cooperative, trusting relationship with one or more colleagues, we advise you to establish one.
—Janet Coster and Milton Schwebel

In addition to your own body signals and personal psychotherapy, your colleagues can play an important role in giving you feedback and support. Both therapists and researchers on practitioner stress consistently advocate talking to your peers as a potent buffer against the hazards of the psychotherapy profession (Dlugos & Friedlander, 2001; Guy, 1987; Maslach, 1982; Norcross, 2000; Yalom, 2002). The therapists I surveyed also cited interaction with other clinicians as one of the most successful tools they had in dealing with work stresses, as well as one of the greatest rewards of being a therapist. These comments are typical of their advice for other mental health workers:

"Form a group of compatible therapists that meets regularly, not only to exchange useful information, but also to validate, support, and care about each other in a confidential setting."

"Talk to other trusted confidants, friends, or therapists as often as possible about patient, practice, or personal concerns."

"Talk to supportive and experienced colleagues, that is, informal consultation."

"Share with your peers."

"Work at developing relationships with colleagues, especially in private practice."

Your peers are very important, both personally and professionally. In addition to socializing, laughing, or complaining together, you can also consult with them and learn from them. As much as possible, make formal and informal use of your colleagues for consultation, interpersonal support, professional development, and networking.

Make Formal and Informal Meetings with Peers Part of Your Regular Schedule

Your coworkers can be an important resource for your guidance and development. If you are working for an agency, much of the support is built in, as you are actively interacting all day long. There are formal staff meetings, as well as informal consultations, where in most instances you need only knock on a door to sound out some ideas, vent, or shoot the breeze. If you are in private practice, you are more likely to become isolated and have to make an active effort to have constant contact with your peers as part of your daily routine.

Although I enjoy being an independent practitioner, there are several aspects of an agency setting that I miss, whether it is the informal lingering by the coffee machine, always having someone to eat lunch with, consulting about different clients at staff meetings, attending regular educational seminars, or simply being able to go to someone's office and chat. I still do many of these things, but I have to work hard at making these part of my regular routine. I need to make certain that they are written into my schedule—they don't happen spontaneously, as they did when I worked in a large organization.

Other therapists who have made the move to private practice also say they miss the socialization and the networking that are automatically built in to other settings. Kottler and Hazler (1997) write that sometimes therapists can spend a whole day seeing only clients and are famished for companionship. They advise making breaks in your day to meet with people, become active in professional organizations, or join a support group. "I feel so isolated and alone," said Heather, a young psychologist and mother who worked part time. "I go to my office, see one client after another, and never talk to anyone else." When I asked Heather why she didn't make time for lunch, professional meetings, or other opportunities for interacting with colleagues, her answer was typical of others I have heard over the years: "I can't afford to. I am only in the office 3 days a week, and any time I spend at work I need to put into client hours. Besides, it takes too much effort. I would have to take time just to arrange it. Plus, everyone else is so busy."

Yes, it does take time; yes, it does take effort; yes, it does take away from client hours. Yet if peer relationships are your life-blood, if they nourish you personally and professionally, you need to carve out room for them and *build them into your regular schedule.* In a previous chapter I discussed how to make your calendar your most important tool. Meetings with other clinicians should be part and parcel of your weekly routine, not only when time allows.

What are some ways to do that? Arrange to have at least one weekly breakfast or lunch with a good friend or a colleague. I am fortunate to have a person who is both in the office next door, and I wouldn't trade our luncheons for anything! At different times, we have had other colleagues join us. This is regularly written into my appointment book, so that I don't have to constantly coordinate or plan. We also go to a place nearby, so that it takes only an hour total. Besides this weekly occurrence, I try to schedule lunches with other people. This may not be as frequent as when I was employed in a large system, but it staves off the isolation.

Besides the weekly noon get-togethers, it is also a good idea to join an association of like-minded therapists, where you can combine socialization and consultation. For many years now, I have been meeting with a small number of clinicians. I look forward to these monthly gatherings—a nice lunch, good company, and a chance to consult and share ideas. If you are not aware of any ongoing groups, you may wish to start one yourself.

There are also many networking breakfasts or luncheons with others who either share your specialty or work in a common geographical area. Whether you meet in someone's house for a potluck meal or at a restaurant, see what you can do to attend. This is one situation where you can combine business with pleasure! Join professional organizations and participate in them!

Some of these associations have an added bonus, in the form of continuing education credits. Another advantage is a chance for networking. If, like Heather, you worry about giving up revenue-generating client hours, having an opportunity to interact with others may in fact bring you more referrals. Try to find a group that meets your needs and *attend meetings regularly!*

Talk to Your Colleagues for Interpersonal Support

One of the memories I have from working at an agency is of a therapist knocking on my door, saying, "I need to scream." She would close the door, let out a big yell, then cheerfully put a big smile on her face, and go out to greet her next client! It's, of course, wonderful to have a place where you can release emotions!

Colleagues can be a resource for venting small frustrations or big ones, often because they are there and can provide you with a listening ear. Many times, they give you more than that—feedback, reassurance, and so much else. Whether it's complaining about insurance companies or trying to deal with the aftermath of a client's suicide, talking to your peers is very helpful. Fellow clinicians can be a source of friendship, support, and regular sharing. In Coster and Schwebel's (1997) study of well-functioning among professional psychologists, peer support was of highest priority for the majority of those studied. Yalom (2002) believes a therapist support group to be a buttress against many of the perils of being a clinician and has attended one for 10 years, consisting of 11 men and meeting every single week.

That a busy professional such as Yalom carves out time regularly to get together with his colleagues attests to the importance of these meetings. It is also not surprising, from what we know about the role of interpersonal support in warding off stress. People who receive a great deal of social support from their friends and coworkers are less upset by life changes and daily hassles (Buunk & Verhoeven, 1991; Roos & Cohen, 1987) and less likely to suffer some of the negative effects of stress (Mallinckrodt & Bennett, 1992).

Utilize Your Colleagues for Consultation and Supervision

Besides providing you with social support, other therapists can be excellent sources of consultation. Conferring about a client with a trusted colleague is like receiving valued supervision. You get to see another perspective and get ideas, particularly when you are feeling stuck or stymied. I have always appreciated the opportunity to discuss specific therapy or practice issues with other clinicians. In fact, psychologists are required to do so under certain situations, and it is always a comfort and a relief to have another opinion.

Consultation and supervision from other practitioners are worthwhile activities. Among the types of advice that experienced counselors would give beginners to help them become happy and effective therapists, getting regular supervision was one of them. Following are some typical responses:

"Get good supervision on a regular basis."

"Get supervision! Regularly!"

"Get peer review."

"Always work under supervision, either in a group practice, through hired supervision, or by a peer supervision arrangement where therapists discuss cases."

In the study of passionately committed therapists (Dlugos & Friedlander, 2001), all but one participant mentioned making use of supervision, either formal or informal. They acknowledged the difficulty, as well as the necessity, of getting appropriate feedback as an independent practitioner. As one therapist put it, "When you work privately, it's much more difficult and, therefore, potentially lethal because supervision is not structured into your day. You've got to make it happen. You've got to make sure. It is lonely. You don't have meetings; you don't see people walking the halls. You have to structure time, where lunch is a chance to talk over an issue that's coming up for you or what a case is about" (p. 301).

As he says, "You've got to make it happen." Having regular meetings with colleagues is one way to do that. Even though you may have already fulfilled the requirements for formal supervision, you might still decide to get supervision on a regular basis as an opportunity to get feedback. Like psychotherapy, frequent supervision and consultation can be ways to "keep you honest," as a colleague put it, and to make sure that your "instrument"—yourself—is clean. It can be particularly useful if you are having uncomfortable feelings about your clients, and it can prevent inappropriate involvement when you are able to openly discuss these feelings (Grosch & Olsen, 1994).

If you are interested in seeking further supervision, your state or local associations can be helpful in supplying information about ongoing groups or clinicians who provide that service. Otherwise, make certain to program built-in opportunities for informal consultation.

Talk to Your Colleagues for Your Own Learning and Professional Development

Supervision, mentoring, seminars, and other forms of training are very important for your professional development, and you can turn to other colleagues for your continued learning and growth. Talking to your peers not only makes you a resilient therapist, it makes you a wise one as well. Consultation, supervision, and attending professional workshops are important for your professional growth. In their study of senior psychotherapists, the authors concluded that to develop optimally, practitioners need to continually reflect on and process both professional and personal experiences. Consultation and supervision are venues for psychotherapists to transform their experiences into wisdom that can be helpful for those they treat (Ronnestad & Skovholt, 2001). Fortunately, most therapists are required to get continuing education and learn from their peers, and you can do your utmost to maximize those opportunities for professional growth.

Over and over, seasoned practitioners have mentioned ongoing learning as important to being a happy and effective therapist, in comments such as these:

"Don't stop putting yourself in situations where you can improve your own insight, get peer review, and keep getting updated in the field."

"Pay attention to continuing medical education opportunities."

"Take training, and self-educate extensively."

"Pursue, most of all, your own growth."

I have already alluded to the value of ongoing learning in previous chapters. Continuing to acquire knowledge is important in preventing burnout, particularly in the stagnation stage, where one of the remedies is further education. Good and happy therapists are constantly evolving and learning, personally and professionally. As George Stricker (2001), a psychologist for nearly 4 decades, writes, the psychotherapist needs "to have the attitude of a scientist . . . and to carry the same attitudes of curiosity, inquisitiveness, dedication and self-reflection into the consulting room that the scientist displays in the laboratory. As long as that attitude can be maintained, learning will continue, and as long as learning continues, both the practice of psychotherapy and the welfare of the patient will be enhanced" (p. 80).

Help Your Colleagues with Their Own Self-Care

The APA Ethics Code (2002) stresses the importance of not only your own self-care but also helping those with whom you work—professional colleagues, as well as clients. The principles of beneficence and nonmaleficence in this code consist of appropriate conduct, ensuring the welfare of those with whom you interact, and educating those people about these matters (Barnett, 2003). What does this translate to in your relationship with colleagues? It means not only helping your associates in their self-care but also doing whatever you can to promote helpful interactions and to do no harm.

When I was a beginning graduate student, a short time after my arrival, the chairman of the psychology department, the late Dr. B. R. Bugelski, stopped me in the hall one day and asked me how I was managing, if I had enough money to cover expenses, and other similar questions to indicate that he cared about my welfare. This incident touched me deeply and obviously left an indelible impression on me because I still remember his kindness nearly 40 years later. He didn't ask about my grades, my achievements, my work—all he was concerned about was my well-being. He cared about *me.*

When I told a colleague that I was writing about therapists' well-being and asked her if she would respond to some questions, she was similarly touched: "You mean someone cares about *us*—not just what we do? We are always taking care of others—no one asks about *us!*"

You can aid your colleagues with their self-care simply by showing an overall interest in their general welfare: "How are you managing?" "Are you okay?" "How are you, *really?*" If you are concerned about them, you can question further: "Are you taking enough time for yourself?" "Are you happy?" "Are you sleeping okay?" "Are you eating okay?" "Can I do anything to help?" These questions are, of course, more appropriate if you are formally supervising someone and have gotten to know him or her well, but even colleagues appreciate your queries if these are not intrusive or patronizing but reflect a genuine caring for them. This may seem elementary, but as the two previous examples illustrate, just asking how they are doing may mean a great deal, in and of itself. Like a well-meaning parent, you are giving the strong underlying message: "I care about you and your welfare." If you are in a formal supervisory or consulting relationship, you can go beyond expressing an interest and educate someone about self-care.

You can help other therapists take care of themselves through both formal and informal channels. Ideally, learning good care habits should begin in graduate school. If you are teaching or supervising students, you can serve as a role model by practicing these habits yourself. For example, you might ask yourself: "What am I teaching my students about self-care if I model a workaholic lifestyle or ask them to adopt one?"

In addition to practicing good health-care habits, you can also demonstrate helpful relationships among colleagues that your trainees can emulate. Setting up an atmosphere of beneficence, which the dictionary defines as "the quality of being kind and charitable," unfortunately does not always characterize interactions among peers, particularly in some settings, where competitiveness, punitiveness, and hostile put-downs are commonplace. Hostile interactions among colleagues are so counterproductive that it has spurred Dr. Robert Sternberg, APA president, to write an article titled "To Be Civil" (2003). As he says, "As a field, we need to set better examples for our colleagues and for the next generation by exerting positive rather than negative leadership, and most importantly, by being civil with those whom we interact" (p. 5).

Caring and respect are the cornerstones of good modeling and mentoring and for teaching your trainees how to care for themselves. It may seem pretty basic and simplistic, but if you treat your supervisees' time as important and their concerns and welfare as serious, they will learn to treat themselves well, too. Sherry frequently asks herself questions such as these in her interactions with her students: "What am I teaching them about their self-worth if I constantly keep them waiting?" "What are they learning about proper professional behavior if I don't return their phone calls promptly?" In other words, she sees her *actions* to be just as important as her words in educating her trainees.

Besides the informal mentoring and role-modeling of good self-care and positive and helpful interactions, you can educate therapists on how they can take care of themselves. If you are a supervisor, I would recommend spending a large amount of time asking and teaching about burnout and sharing some of the benefits of your experience. You can also help your trainees monitor how many hours they work, ask if they are getting enough "I" time, and observe for signs of the overresponsibility trap or for symptoms of burnout.

If you are a student or a newcomer, don't be afraid to ask for specific information on the subject. If you don't have a "built-in" mentor, one who cares about your welfare and who takes you under his or her wing, do whatever you can to find one, whether in a supervisory capacity or through a therapist who can help you develop long-term healthy habits. The time to do this is now and not after you burn out or decide to leave the field altogether. I is hoped that you will have several helpful mentoring relationships during your professional development. For more information on the many benefits of mentoring, which include better training, career success, and professional identity, as well as on how to go about finding a mentor and getting the most out of that experience, you might wish to read *Getting Mentored in Graduate School* (2003) by W. Brad Johnson and Jennifer M. Huwe.

Ideally, the teaching of burnout avoidance should be mandatory and a formal part of training. In my opinion, not only should training programs educate about healthy self-care habits, they also need to follow through with action. What messages are we giving therapists-in-training, for example, when we routinely ask them to work 60 or more hours a week, when they are kept so busy every waking moment, when they have no time for a "life," for sleep, or for little else? As a colleague once told me, "We spend all these years dehumanizing them and then expect them to wake up, years later, like Rip Van Winkle, and become human again." It would be important to structure training programs so that the years spent in graduate schools, internships, and residency programs are not seen as periods of incarceration before getting a life.

What should you do if you are not in a supervisory position with another therapist and you notice signs of burnout? How can you aid other professional colleagues who seem to be in need of self-care and don't recognize it? The problem is more tricky, because you may not want to be seen as intrusive, yet at the same time you are concerned. Approach this as you would any situation when you see a problem with someone you care about. "I've noticed such and such," you might say. "Are you all right?" Sharing some of your own experiences may be very helpful in giving your colleagues permission to acknowledge the problem. Often, a few suggestions on ways of ameliorating work stress (or giving them a copy of this book!) may be all that is necessary. However, if you sense that the problem is deeper than that, encourage them to see a therapist.

Sherman and Thelen (1998) provide the following guidelines for helping impaired or distressed colleagues at a broader level. They state that because most people will experience some major personal or work stresses at different parts of their lives, training programs can be proactive in preparing trainees for how to cope effectively at those times. The education can be in the form of mandatory workshops, ethics courses, or clinical practicum. The mandated training can continue afterward, either in continuing education courses or through state licensure boards, which would make that a requirement for renewing licenses. Organizations that hire therapists may also mandate training on professional distress and impairment for new employees at orientation and can offer similar continuing education classes for all employees. In addition, they can impose a preexisting system for dealing with distressed therapists, such as decreasing their responsibilities at this time or increasing support from colleagues. The issue of therapist self-care is very important and needs attention at all levels.

The subject of impaired clinicians is beyond the scope of this book but is sufficiently significant that the American Psychological Association formulated a response emphasizing both education and prevention, with state associations assuming responsibility for developing intervention programs. For more on this topic, refer to *Assisting Impaired Psychologists* (1994) by Milton Schwebel, Jane Skorina, and Gary Schoenor.

To sum up this chapter, talk to your colleagues—regularly—for your own well-being and theirs and for that of your clients.

Self-Assessment

Are formal and informal meetings with my peers part of my regular schedule?

If not, how can I build them into it on a regular basis? Check all that apply.

_____ Having a weekly breakfast or lunch together

_____ Joining an association of like-minded therapists that meets on a regular basis

_____ Getting regular supervision or consultation, formal or informal

_____ Attending seminars and other opportunities for learning on a regular basis

_____ (Other) ____

What concrete steps do I need to take to build these activities into my regular schedule?

What are some ways I can help other therapists with their own self-care?

CHAPTER 19

Get Out of the Overresponsibility Trap

You didn't cause it. You can't fix it. Take care of yourself.
—Nancy Zimbro, social worker

One of the traps that many clinicians, particularly beginning ones, get into that contributes to burnout is that of trying to be all things to all people and assuming a *tremendous* amount of responsibility for the outcome of psychotherapy. This is also sometimes referred to as the supertherapist trap or the rescuer trap and goes something like this: "If I were a really good ("super," "knew what I was doing," etc.) therapist, my client would improve," or conversely, "If my client isn't getting better, I must be doing something wrong." There is obviously some truth to these statements at times. "Good" therapists will likely have better outcomes than "bad" therapists, in most cases. However, it is the *disproportionate* amount of responsibility that you take for your clients' welfare that contributes not only to your own burnout but to the detriment of those you treat as well.

"No One Is Indispensable"

A supervisor once said those words to me, words I repeat often to other therapists and supervisees when they are engaging in too much caregiving and bearing a great deal of the load for their patients. The overresponsibility trap can also take the form of "I am the only one who can take care of this client" or "I need to be available at all times to meet my patients' needs."

Some authors suggest that behind this overcaretaking may be a "masked narcissism," a belief that you are special and more important than you really are (Grosch & Olsen, 1994; Welt & Herron, 1990). The caretaking may also be a carryover of family-of-origin issues, with therapists falling back to a familiar role (Guy, 1987) and other unconscious motivations (Sussman, 1992). Whatever the origins, learn to recognize when you are engaging in too much caretaking and take appropriate steps to let go.

Lydia, a psychologist, found herself feeling exhausted, drained, and frustrated. It seemed to her that she was constantly talking to her clients, returning emergency phone calls at all hours, and feeling as if she had no life of her own. In her spare time, she worried about clients and how they were doing. "I am suffering from caregiver burnout," she said. She saw no way out of the trap—she was their therapist, and they needed her and depended on her to get them through, from one crisis to another. If you find yourself working harder than your patients and putting in too much actual and emotional "overtime" between sessions, you are likely assuming too much responsibility for their well-being and depriving them of doing some of the work themselves. If you are *too* invested in the outcome of a particular therapy case, again you may be taking on a burden that isn't yours.

The research shows that new practitioners, in particular, tend to be overinvolved in their clients' progress and to assume more responsibilities (Skovholt & Ronnestad, 2001). Many beginning therapists start out with a rescuer fantasy, that through their therapeutic skills, empathy, and caring, the client will make dramatic changes. They tell themselves that if they persist enough, if they are always available, or if they say the right words, they will magically transform their patients' long-term patterns and produce life-altering changes. They will work harder and harder than their clients and let their clients' crises become their own. They start assuming more and more responsibility for the welfare of those who come to them for help and end up feeling discouraged, burned out, and angry when their heroic efforts and hard labor seem to be in vain.

The overresponsibility trap may be more pronounced for beginning therapists for several reasons. Inexperienced clinicians can easily overestimate their capacity and start off too fast. Newcomers are also uncertain about what is realistic and may make the error of believing their interventions can bring change more quickly and completely than is possible. Fortunately, Skovholt and Ronnestad's (2001) findings suggest that as practitioners gain more experience, they are more able to assume appropriate responsibility.

Watch out for instances of overcaretaking in your interactions. When you find yourself taking over, pay attention to your mood. When you catch yourself feeling depleted or resentful, see if you have been engaging in rescuing behaviors. No one is indispensable—nor should be. If you think you are the only one who can help your client, if you believe that he or she can't make it without your constant micromanaging, then you are getting yourself into the overresponsibility trap—one that is causing you burnout and fostering dependency in your clients.

Set Realistic Expectations

The overresponsibility trap stems from a kind of therapist perfectionism and setting impossible goals for yourself, your clients, and the process of therapy. Perfectionism among clinicians is quite common and can also reduce your enjoyment of your work. In a study of nearly 200 private practice psychologists, whose mean age was 52 years, it was found that perfectionism and low tolerance for ambiguity can decrease the satisfaction of conducting therapy (Wittenberg & Norcross, 2001). If you observe yourself engaging in too much caretaking and putting more and more work into your clients, only to end up feeling frustrated, you probably have some unrealistic expectations of yourself and of psychotherapy in general.

For starters, as one clinician advised, "Don't fear your competency because you don't know 'everything,' and don't expect to be 'all things to all people.'" George Stricker (2001), a psychologist with many years of experience, in his reflections about being a psychotherapist, put it this way: ". . . perfection and certainty are impossible and . . . we therapists must do the best we can and be content to be 'good enough'" (p. 80).

You may know this intellectually; however, there may be that other voice that says, "Yes, but I *should* be able to . . ." Tell those "shoulds" to get lost! If you are a new therapist, it will take you at least 5 to 10 years to start feeling comfortable conducting therapy. Even if you are an experienced clinician, there will be many times when you feel like you don't know what you are doing or feel stuck. If you are telling yourself, "I *should* know this" or "I *should* be able to change his behavior" or are engaging in other types of "should" statements, it is a good idea to examine those beliefs and focus instead on what is within your control.

As a therapist suggests in her advice for beginning practitioners, "You didn't cause it. You can't fix it. Take care of yourself." This, of course, is not to say that you or your interventions are not relevant to the treatment outcome. Psychotherapy is teamwork, and even if your suggestions are ingenious, they cannot do any good unless the client actively utilizes them. As Arthus Bohart (2001), an integrative-existential therapist, states, ". . . the brilliance of the intervention did not matter until the client decided to use it" (p. 238). He goes on to add that whereas many books on the therapeutic process depict the therapist as the hero, *the client is the ultimate agent of change.* Clients are not dependent variables on whom you impose treatments, as in medicine: They are collaborators who bring your therapy to life. The overwhelming conclusion is, ". . . the client, not the therapist, is the engine that drives the therapy. The therapist provides structure, tools and a good working environment. The most important variable in therapy is not client diagnosis or therapist intervention, but client involvement and participation" (p. 237).

What does this mean for you? It means to be realistic about how much of an impact you can have on those who come to you with their problems. A therapist's job is sometimes not unlike a diplomatic mediator trying to impose peace between two warring nations. Regardless of the sophistication of the negotiator's skills or the soundness of the peace plan, no change can be effected unless the parties want to implement it. Just as the diplomat didn't cause the hostilities between the two countries, you didn't bring on your clients' problems. They had a history long before you came into the picture.

Setting realistic goals for change also means knowing what the parameters are. A colleague who works with severely depressed and suicidal patients has as her goal simply to have them stay alive. To return to the diplomat analogy, a pragmatic goal may be just maintaining the status quo and keeping the enemies from starting a nuclear war. A therapist of several severely psychotic clients counts as her successes keeping them out of the hospital. A psychologist who works with brain-injured individuals knows what she can or cannot do. She cannot reverse the brain injury, but she can provide ongoing support for the families. A grief counselor cannot take away the pain and the sadness from the mourner but can provide a safe, comfortable environment to discharge feelings. Remember, you are not responsible for the problems. You didn't cause them, and you cannot magically take them away. Setting realistic goals means being accountable only for yourself and not for the actions of your clients. You can stand on your head for hours on end, but your patients won't make any movements until they decide to. Focus only on what you can control.

Setting attainable goals also applies to the therapy experience. If you wait for those magical "Aha!" Perry Mason–type moments, when your clients have an epiphany and alter their whole lives as a result, you will be sadly disappointed. Most change is slow and not very dramatic. As Morris Eagle (2001), a psychoanalyst, puts it in his reflections as a therapist: "Apocalyptic and unrealistic goals, such as personality transformation and rebirth, do the patient a disservice because, among other things, they trivialize more realistic and more modest accomplishments, which, albeit modest, make an important difference in a person's life" (p. 52).

Don't look for *huge* changes right away, but note the *small,* incremental successes. A client who has difficulty saying hello to others will not metamorphose into an extrovert overnight. For your sake—and his—it is important to reinforce the minor attainments along the way to the larger goal. As one therapist advised, "Avoid judging success by 'cures.'"

Keep a time perspective. Chances are, when you think of persons you have seen for many years, you may remember the gains they have made from the time they began treatment. Some patients take giant leaps—others, baby steps. A time line helps you to have a perspective on progress. Don't expect results right away. Many people take months or even years to make significant shifts in their lives, and their course involves a series of mini-steps along the way.

Having realistic goals in therapy also means highlighting the successes and not the failures. If you engage in perfectionistic thinking, you will no doubt linger on the mistakes. It is important instead to look at what's working and emphasize the "wins." Similarly, you will want to focus on the *process* of therapy, rather than on the outcome. The satisfaction is in the doing, not in the end result.

Setting achievable goals means not taking what happens personally. You didn't get people depressed or anxious, and you are not responsible for "fixing" them. If clients don't improve in spite of your best efforts, use it as an opportunity for further learning. Yes, maybe you could have done some things better, but make sure you were not shooting for the moon. Have realistic expectations of yourself, of your clients, and of the therapy process to avoid the overresponsibility trap.

If you are still having difficulty letting go, remind yourself of some of the hazards of setting unreasonably high goals in general, which include depression, anxiety, impaired health, and less productivity (Burns, 1980). The risks of placing unrealistic demands on yourself or your clients can be equally diastrous. Professionals who are overly idealistic, with unusually high expectations of what they can achieve, are at a very high risk of being burned out (Farber, 1983; Guy, 1987), as well as of living a frenetic lifestyle (Grosch & Olsen, 1994). In a series of essays written by psychotherapists who had experienced major depression, most of these practitioners said they would do things differently and would have more realistic expectations of what they could achieve (Rippere & Williams, 1985). I would encourage you to learn from their experience!

Don't Work Harder Than Your Client

Many years ago, I was seeing a woman in therapy—I'll call her Ella—who came in week after week to complain about her husband. George was so fat, ugly, repulsive, and abusive—at least, to her—that she couldn't stand to be in the same room with him. She was so miserable in her marriage, she didn't know how she could take it another moment. She just needed the courage to leave and didn't know how she could do that. I listened and listened and got more and more incensed as I heard about George's horrific behavior. I couldn't see why anyone should have to put up with such actions, and I did everything in my power to rescue her from this "monster," including—I'm embarrassed to say—giving her the name of a divorce attorney. Ella did leave George—17 years later when he walked out on her. I heard this through the grapevine after I had stopped seeing Ella. What did I learn from this? I was overinvested in Ella's marriage, and I was exerting myself more than she was. I was more set on her leaving George than she was! I was doing all the work for her and feeling frustrated that she wasn't moving!

The client should do at least 90% of the work in therapy. If you find yourself putting in more energy than your client, then you are bearing a disproportionate amount of the load and also fostering dependency in the process. Lydia, who was "burned out from caretaking," made a detailed list of all that she considered her obligations at work. After she studied the items, she realized that she was assuming responsibility for tasks that belonged to her clients or her colleagues, doing things for them that they could easily do themselves, and feeling burdened and resentful. Lydia, for example, called her patients to remind them about appointments, something that was clearly their job. She also frequently took on the role of messenger and talked to their families, their doctors, or whomever they were having trouble with, often intervening in situations that were outside her control and none of her business. She was constantly trying to "fix" their problems for them. She also recognized that she was doing tasks for coworkers who were taking advantage of her because she was so conscientious and dependable.

Lydia was horrified to see how much responsibility she was taking on that was not hers. Stephen Covey, in a speech on effective management, tells the story of a manager who takes on his employees' problems, or "monkeys." His subordinates come to his office, one at a time. "Hey, boss, I wasn't able to make that phone call." "No problem. I'll do it." "Hey, boss, I don't know how to do this." "Just put it on my desk, and I'll deal with it." The employees keep dropping their "monkeys" in the supervisor's lap. At the end of the day, they all leave for home, whereas he sits in his office until all hours taking care of their "monkeys." Don't take on anyone else's monkeys! Give them right back. Otherwise, you will be like the manager working late into the night, while others go home relaxed and carefree, knowing that their work is being taken care of.

Although it is admirable to want to help and "go the extra mile," being overresponsible actually robs your clients of learning to stand on their own two feet and gives them the impression that they can't take care of themselves. A proverb says, "Don't give me fish. Teach me how to fish." Overinvolved therapists who constantly spoonfeed their patients instead of providing them with the skills to do that themselves are similar to parents who take responsibility for their children's school assignments ("*We* have homework to do") and even, at times, do the assignments for the child! This may work in the short run—it may result in a better grade—but it shortchanges the kids in the long haul, depriving them of the opportunity to learn to do the job themselves and of the sense of accomplishment that goes with it.

Indeed, a psychotherapist's job is not unlike a parent's. Therapy and parenthood are the only two occupations where your ultimate goal is to work yourself out of a job. Although it may feel good to be needed, you are not going to be around forever, and your aim is to help your clients—or kids—learn to make it on their own. Assuming too much responsibility—by doing the work for them that they should be doing themselves—only gives them the message that they are not capable and creates further dependency.

Learn to let go and allow clients to steer through the course of psychotherapy in their own manner. The more you do, the less they do, as I found out the hard way with Ella. Let them do the work, instead of doing it for them. This doesn't mean not being active or engaged. It doesn't mean not going the extra mile to help them feel comfortable. It doesn't mean being inaccessible. It just means giving them the opportunity to accomplish the task themselves and have the satisfaction of knowing they can.

Assume the role of a coach, a teacher, or a consultant, rather than an expert "fixer" or "rescuer." Let your clients know immediately that *they*—and not you—are the ultimate agents of change, and convey that message in word and deed. As noted previously in this chapter, the most important determinant of progress is the *client's* participation in therapy, and it is the *client*, more than you, who implements this process. The more psychotherapists have depended on the clients' resources, the more change occurs (Bohart, 2001). Remember that the next time you are tempted to "over-caregive."

As Janet Pipal (1997) says in one of her spiritual truths for clinicians, people will rise or sink to your expectations of them. If you constantly "spoonfeed" your patients, they will feel helpless and incapable of taking care of themselves. You may wish to explain what you're doing if you decide to stop being so "helpful." You may also be surprised—sometimes those individuals whom you think are least able to manage can do so when you stop taking care of them!

As much as possible, try to let go; the more you attempt to control the therapy process and the more you are invested in the outcome—as I was with Ella—the more frustrated you will feel. And remember, feeling resentment toward your client is not therapeutic! Other therapists (Mahoney, 2001) have frequently spoken about learning to relinquish control as a factor in their growth as therapists: ". . . I began to relax some of my needs to understand everything that was taking place in my life and in my clients' lives" (p. 194) and ". . . I am more patient now and much more tolerant of ambiguity. I am not in as much of a hurry to change clients' presenting concerns" (p. 198).

I learned with Ella to allow clients to navigate therapy themselves in their own way and on their own time table. Arthur Kovaks, a psychologist, gives, as a tip for thriving and surviving in today's practice, letting patients end therapy in their own manner: "Don't push clients to stay longer than they want to, and let them choose the way they leave—whether it's by a long, anguished letting-go, or an abrupt leave-taking. As they go, gently plant seeds for change, with the hope they'll germinate later with you or a colleague. But release your clients freely" (1997, p. 17).

Getting out of the overresponsibility trap means letting go—letting go of unrealistic expectations of yourself, of your clients, and of therapy and letting go of the need to control those things you can't in the psychotherapeutic process.

Self-Assessment

The following are some thoughts and behaviors associated with the overresponsibility trap.

Which of these indicators apply to me? Check all that apply.

_____ Being overinvested in the therapy outcome

_____ Feeling drained and exhausted

_____ Working harder than my clients

_____ Putting in too much emotional or actual "overtime" between sessions

_____ Allowing my clients' crises to become my own

_____ Assuming responsibilities for others that they can do themselves

_____ Doing more than 50% of the work in therapy

_____ Feeling like I am the only one who can help my clients

_____ Micromanaging a great deal

_____ Feeling resentful when my clients don't show progress in spite of my efforts

_____ Frequently engaging in "should" statements where it concerns my clients (e.g., "I *should* be able to help him" etc.)

_____ Looking for big changes right away

_____ Focusing on the failures verus the successes

_____ Taking what happens in therapy very personally

_____ Engaging in rescuing behaviors

_____ (Other) ____

If you are engaging in any of these behaviors or if overcaretaking is a problem for you, the following activity, adapted from Melody Beattie (1987), may be helpful for you. Write down all the things you consider your responsibilities at work.

My Responsibilities:

Now list in detail what responsibilities belong to the other people in your work, including your clients and colleagues.

Other People's Responsibilities:

Am I taking on too much responsibility that properly belongs to others?

If yes, what steps do I need to take to get out of the overresponsibility trap?

CHAPTER 20

Keep a Healthy Distance

To provide the best—whether it be service, care, treatment or education—the helper should use both objective detachment and sensitive concern, rather than choosing one over the other.
—Christina Maslach, *Burnout: The Cost of Caring*

In Chapter 12 I discussed the importance of putting a line of demarcation between your professional and your private lives as a way to manage your outer environment. In this chapter, I will talk about setting boundaries *within* your inner environment and learning to maintain a healthy distance between the emotional demands of your work and your personal life. When you immerse yourself, day in and day out, in the internal worlds of distressed individuals, it is bound to take a psychological toll on you (Sussman, 1995). There is a paradox in being a therapist. On the one hand, you need to be caring and empathetic for your clients; on the other hand, you must have some objectivity to be effective.

What is an optimal distance? It is one where you feel safe to be yourself and where your client also feels safe. Some detachment is necessary for your well-being and for that of the person coming to you for help. A psychotherapy relationship is one of mutual respect and trust, and if neither of you feels safe, then it cannot be therapeutic. A healthy distance is not so close that you lose your perspective, not so close that you lose your mental health, and, in extreme cases, not so close that it threatens your physical safety. It is also not so close that your client feels unsafe, by thinking either that it would be too much for you, that you can't handle it, that you are too involved to be objective, or that you are so far removed, you don't care. Regardless of theoretical orientation, some detachment is necessary for therapists to maintain perspective enough to gain insight and understanding (Guy, 1987).

Paula's work with a child who was abused and who threatened suicide brought up memories of her own childhood. "I don't want to go there," she said. She could recognize her feelings and worked through them in therapy. She could also recognize her limits. If her emotions were too painful for her, then she may not be able to be of any value—to herself or to her client. Although her empathy helped her to feel and "get it" quickly, she didn't have the emotional distance to know what "normal" was. For example, when she related to her colleague the father's treatment of the child, the coworker was aghast. Paula did not know enough to be shocked or to know what that meant. She was too "close" and didn't have the objectivity to properly evaluate and assess the situation.

How do you continue to be an active, concerned, warm human being and stay detached at the same time? In this chapter, I will discuss ways of keeping a healthy emotional space, while remaining nurturant and empathetic.

Recognize the Hazards of Being a Therapist

As John Norcross (2000) states as foremost in his practitioner-tested, research-based strategies for clinicians, begin by saying out loud, "Psychotherapy is often a grueling and demanding calling." We have already seen the pressures involved in being a therapist. Recognize this fact and acknowledge it. When you realize that stress is inherent in the work you do and that nearly all practitioners experience some form of distress, that in itself can be therapeutic and can also lead to taking some steps to decrease the inevitable emotional toll that is part of your job.

No matter how much you may try to discount it, you cannot listen to people's problems all day long without some of their turmoil rubbing off on you. If you can accept that fact, then you affirm the need to keep a healthy distance—midway between being overinvolved and being aloof—between your emotions and those of your clients.

Why do you need to keep some space? First of all, you must separate yourself for your own sake, to avoid burnout and compassion fatigue. Second, you need to develop some detachment for the sake of your patients. "I never tell my mom anything," a young man confided in me. "She gets more upset than I do." You don't want your clients to feel that you will be more shaken than they are or that they cannot talk to you because you can't handle it. If you want to set up an atmosphere where people feel comfortable discussing anything on their minds, it is important to have some emotional removal for their benefit.

Don't Allow Your Clients' Crises To Become Yours

When I was doing my internship, I counseled a young man whose family seemed to have a life-and-death crisis every week. I held my breath each time he recounted the incidents and prayed that nothing terrible would happen. My emotions went up and down like a roller coaster with the events that unfolded in this family. One day my supervisor took me aside and said something to this effect: "In your house or my house, if these episodes occurred, they might be considered crises. To your client, this is a way of life. To him, it is not a crisis, but to you, it is." I took his advice to heart and have repeated his words to many of the clinicians I have mentored. Don't let your clients' crises become your own. Or, in other words, don't get more upset about the events in their lives than they are themselves. You may be much more distressed than they are.

In the last chapter, I stressed the value of having a historical perspective on your patients' progress. A time line keeps the problem in focus and prevents you from blowing it out of proportion. Seeing the crisis in the context of many other such incidents helps diffuse it for you. Many therapists report that they frequently feel very distressed by the end of a heart-wrenching session. They enter the next meeting with dread, anticipating further emotional trauma, only to discover that the client has already let go of what took place the week before and is focused on something else. Having a time perspective gives you some distance from the problem and enables you to see it as part of a larger pattern, keeping it in the background, rather than looming in the foreground. Learn to see the problem in a broader context, rather than having myopic vision. Look at the big picture.

I recall when I saw my first bulimic client many years ago. She was so depressed and hopeless that within a few minutes, I found my mood going further and further downhill with each word she said. I got more and more pessimistic. How was I ever going to intervene in her hopeless cycle? When I left the session and had an opportunity to gain some distance, I recognized that I had one of two choices: I could let her bring me down emotionally or I could try to bring her up. As I retreated and got some perspective, I could focus on the process of what was happening. The woman was engaging in some of the most negative thinking I had ever heard! Once I became aware of her cognitions, I could show her what she was doing. Not surprisingly, she started paying attention to and changing her thought patterns. Since that time, I have seen many bulimic patients who also initially started out with hopeless, helpless thinking. When I am able to stand back and point out the process to them, instead of getting hooked into their negativity, I can be much more helpful to them.

If you find your moods going up and down with your clients', step back and concentrate on what they are doing to feel so distressed. This provides you with the emotional distance to remain unruffled and helps them gain some perspective as well. You need to be more composed than they are, or their crises become more intensified. When I was doing some work at a suicide prevention center, we used to joke that when the phone rang, there were two people in crisis: the caller and the therapist! Calmness on your part is essential. If both of you panic, the client is really in trouble!

"I remember once when I was really having a hard time," said Lynette. "I actually thought I was losing my mind and going crazy. I felt dizzy and thought I was going to faint. I was so scared, I didn't even know what to do. My heart was pounding, and I felt like I was losing control. I could hear the panic in my husband's voice and in the tone of all the people around me. I picked up the phone and called my therapist. I could hear her calm, steadfast voice, so unlike all the others. I held on to the phone for dear life. She seemed composed and unruffled. Her reassuring tone immediately put me at ease. I knew I was going to be okay, that I wasn't losing my mind. She kept her serene, steady, reassuring tone throughout." At no time are emotional distance and calmness more important than in a crisis to help clients feel safe.

Keep Clear Boundaries between You and Your Clients

As I mentioned in Chapter 12, Janet Pipal's (1997) first of 10 spiritual truths is that good boundaries are holy—boundaries between home and work and between you and your client. Aside from the ethical and the legal mandates of having boundaries between you and your clients, limits are important for the orderly progression of therapy. Weinberg, in his book *The Heart of Psychotherapy* (1984), cites the therapist's separateness as one of the main criteria for psychotherapy to be effective. Not only is the lack of good boundarids harmful to you, but it can also compromise your stance as a therapist and adversely affect your clients, particularly if the crossings turn into boundary violations (Gabbard & Lester, 1995; Lamb, Catanzaro, & Moorman, 2003; Pope, 1990; Reamer, 2001). And as I mentioned in Chapter 15, research shows that when therapists are most burned out, they are more likely to engage in inappropriate behaviors or make decisions that hurt their clients.

Here is some of the advice given by seasoned therapists to beginning practitioners:

> "Keep clear boundaries between yourself as a professional and patients or clients whose welfare and safety depend on your expertise in this area."

> "Friendship with clients should be avoided."

Setting clear boundaries with clients at the outset of therapy about mutually expected behavior is important, as discussed in Chapter 12. The boundaries between practitioners and their patients are clearly outlined in guidelines for mental health professionals: no dual relationships between therapists and clients (American Psychological Association, 2002). That means no sex, no socializing, no dating, no business ventures together, and no accepting of bribes or gifts. Most of the time, these rules are clear and cut-and-dried. However, what about the gray areas? What happens if you are at a conference where your client, another therapist, is also attending and you are seated at the same table for lunch? What happens if you live in a small town and get invited to the same places? These and other sticky situations crop up from time to time. In a national survey of 1,319 psychologists, the most frequently described ethical dilemmas involved confidentiality and maintaining clear boundaries around the professional relationship with a client (Pope & Vetter, 1992).

When I was a beginning therapist, one of my clients, a shy, introverted woman, brought me a present—a large batch of cookies that she had baked. I knew what the rules were—no gifts from patients, ever. I had it so hammered into me that receiving anything from a client was a no-no that I said I couldn't accept them. One look at her face told me that I had made a foolish mistake. My client was offering me a token of her feelings for me, and I was stupidly rejecting what she wanted to give me. I immediately knew I had made a terrible error by sticking to the letter of the law rather than the spirit, forgetting the human connection that is the essence of a therapeutic relationship. I was engaging in black-and-white thinking, with nearly disastrous results.

Presents can be murky areas, and judgment is called for in assessing whether accepting them crosses clear boundaries (Lyckhom, 1998; Polster, 2001). The guideline I use is: Is this for the client's benefit or for mine? Obviously, if it is a small gift, particularly something that the person coming for therapy has made, to show appreciation and to remember him or her by, I accept it warmly. A heart-shaped paperweight on my desk, a tiny box, a plant, a flower, a poem, a drawing, or anything small and symbolic of the therapeutic relationship—these I receive gratefully, knowing that they are tangible representations of appreciation. If the gift is clearly inappropriate, I would, of course, reject it, although I have to say that this has never happened in the entire time that I have been in practice. Nobody has ever offered me—or, as far as I know, any other therapist—a diamond broach, a Porsche, a fur coat, a trip to Hawaii, or anything else with an embarrassingly high monetary value. The presents have been small, meaningful objects that I keep to remember the clients long after termination. They are truly gifts of the heart. Talk to your clients about the meaning of the gift when you are uncertain about appropriateness.

My views on gifts are shared by most mental health professionals. In a large national survey of psychologists, psychiatrists, and social workers, only a tiny minority believed that accepting gifts under $10 was unethical, and the majority had done it (Bory & Pope, 1989). One of the most widely read and cited ethics textbooks in psychology (Koocher & Keith-Spiegel, 1998) states that accepting small material tokens, such as homemade cookies or an inexpensive gift, typically poses no ethical problem. When a gift is no longer "small," it constitutes a therapeutic issue.

Although the rules are very definite about no socialization with people you counsel, some situations require judgment. If an invitation from a patient is clearly outside the boundaries ("Let's have dinner"), it is easy to explain that this is not allowed in the psychotherapy profession. However, some circumstances are not as clear-cut, and you can use the same guidelines as with gifts. If you choose to attend a social funcion, *do it for the client's benefit and so that it helps him or her.* The event should have therapeutic value and be symbolic of some of the work you have done in therapy. It would also be helpful to discuss with the client beforehand how you would handle confidentiality and privacy in those situations.

What are examples of those events? On three occasions, I have attended clients' weddings when I had seen them intensively for premarital counseling. Getting married was a reflection of their accomplishment in the therapy process. In all of these cases, I said that I didn't want my presence to cause them embarrassment, but they stated that it wouldn't and said they wanted me to come. I felt that not attending would be seen as a rejection and would be counterproductive. I have also gone to a party celebrating a woman's 5-year survival from cancer, a clear symbol of the work she had done in therapy. Other instances may be going to a client's opening at an art gallery, a play, a patient's funeral where the family knows you, or any other event where your attendance is *for the sake of your client and a part of the therapeutic work you have been doing together.* The function should be an extension of therapy, rather than for your own socialization needs.

Any time you go to a social gathering where your client is present, you run the risk of violating confidentiality. The person may choose to introduce you as his or her therapist, but what happens if others ask you how you know each other? One time I ran into a woman at a reception. The man with her asked us how we had met. My quick-thinking client said, "Oh, here and there." I have remembered her response and use it on such occasions.

There may be times when you are inadvertently thrown into situations where you will be socializing or conducting business with your patients, particularly if they are therapists themselves or if you live in a small town (Campbell & Gordon, 2003; Solomon, Heisberger, & Winer, 1981). In those instances, it is fairly easy to keep the professional aspects of the relationship separate from the therapy ones. For example, you could both be on the same panel and be seated at lunch or dinner together with other colleagues without needing to disclose how you know each other and thereby compromising confidentiality.

At other times, this can be trickier. Several years ago, I was seeing a graduate student in therapy. I was also teaching a practicum course at the university, when I found out that I had been assigned to supervise this particular woman. I was in a bind. Of course, I couldn't say that she was my client, and at the same time, I couldn't be supervising someone who was coming to me for counseling. I talked to a trusted colleague on how to handle this situation, and we decided I would talk to my client about it. Fortunately, the student chose to bring this up herself with her adviser, and she got another faculty member to supervise her.

Self-disclosure is another area where the limits aren't always so clear, and its therapeutic value, as well as its pitfalls, are summarized by several therapists (Kottler, 1993; Yalom, 2002). Research suggests that clients experience both positive and negative consequences as a result of their therapists' self-disclosure (Peterson, 2002). Although it may be helpful in the immediate process of therapy, its effects on ultimate outcome are less clear (Hill & Knox, 2001).

How much of yourself do you reveal and still have some boundaries? Although a great deal depends on your own theoretical orientation and views of therapy, the guidelines for gifts and social events apply here, too. A useful tip is to reveal personal information only when it is expressly for the client's benefit, for example, "When I feel . . . , I find it helpful to . . ." This type of statement can help normalize the client's feelings and suggests ways of coping. If you choose to talk about yourself, do not go into unnecessary details and talk only about resolved issues, rather than unresolved ones. Remember, this is the client's hour! If you choose to self-disclose, do it only because you think it will help your client in therapy.

George Weinberg, in his book *The Heart of Psychotherapy* (1984), cautions about the risks of self-disclosure: "A good principle is that it's never wrong not to talk about ourselves, and it is often wrong to do" (p. 245). Peter Gruenberg (2001), a psychiatrist writing on boundary violations for the American Psychiatric Association, puts it even more succinctly: "The best advice continues to be: *When in doubt, don't*" (p. 5).

Describing the many "gray areas" in boundary setting is beyond the scope of this book. For more information on the topic, you can refer to *Tangled Relationships* (Reamer, 2001), *Boundaries and Boundary Violations in Psychoanalysis* (Gabbard & Lester, 1995), or *Ethics in Psychology: Professional Standards and Cases* (Koocher & Keith-Spiegel, 1998). It is always prudent to consult other professionals when you are uncertain what to do. A therapist who was retiring wasn't sure how to handle her patient's request that they become friends now that there was no longer going to be a formal psychotherapeutic relationship. She discussed this with her peers and used them as a sounding board to get feedback, just as I had done when I felt in a bind between my role as a therapist and that of a supervisor. When you are not sure what the boundaries are—what a healthy distance is—talk to your colleagues!

Keep a Sense of Humor

One of the best ways to keep your perspective is through laughter. In fact, maintaining a sense of humor was endorsed by more clinicians than any other coping strategy for dealing with occupational stress. Fully 82% of psychotherapists listed it as a career-sustaining behavior (Kramen-Kahn & Hansen, 1998), and it is effective in modulating burnout when working with trauma (Moran, 2002). Alan Klein, in his book *The Courage to Laugh* (1998), describes the healing effects of humor, even in the grief process: "It is nature's way of giving us a perspective on a situation and allowing us to rise above it. Humor helps us keep our balance when life throws us a curve ball" (p. 4).

Humor helps you detach from a situation—at least, temporarily—and maintain your balance. It keeps you from getting caught up in the moment-to-moment details of a dilemma. It prevents you from wallowing in the sadness and hopelessness of something and losing sight of the bigger picture. When you step back from the problem a little, it may not be as gloomy as you thought.

Humor distracts and diverts your attention and allows you not to take yourself so seriously, especially during difficult times. In addition, the laughter can release pent-up emotion and can enable you to discuss taboo subjects. I recall a client who was dying of cancer and I roaring hysterically when she told me that her sisters had been upset that she had made arrangements to be buried in an expensive dress, instead of saving her good clothes! Another woman with cancer was often asked, "Are you Orthodox?" because she wore a turban. Her reply: "No, I'm Chemothox!"

When you can laugh about something serious, it diffuses the matter and provides hope. Laughter is partly an escape from reality, a "getting away from it all"; partly a release of tension, and partly a way to see a situation differently. Humor may not change the circumstances, but it is a way of reframing something. When you focus on the absurdities of an issue, this provides the chance—for you and for your clients—to step back and gain a healthy distance from the problem at hand.

Laughing with colleagues has been one of the most enjoyable aspects of working in an agency. When we could see the absurdities underneath even the most difficult situations, we were able to let out a great deal of tension. Of course, humor can backfire if you are having a joke at someone else's expense or if it is disrespectful. However, laughter is a way for you to create the emotional distance necessary to detach somewhat and not get engulfed in a problem.

Learn To Recognize and Avoid Vicarious Traumatization

Nowhere is maintaining a healthy distance more important than when seeing clients who have experienced significant ordeals—accidents, assaults, and other tragedies. "Vicarious traumatization," the enduring deleterious effects of trauma therapy on the clinician, occurs when therapists vicariously experience the stresses of those they treat (Pearlman & Saakvitne, 1995). Many counselors start to feel their own sense of loss or stress when working with clients who have suffered traumatic losses. The effects of working with trauma survivors can be acute, especially for counselors who have experienced similar ordeals themselves (Pearlman & MacIan, 1995). However, even practitioners without any trauma history are susceptible to experiencing severe reactions. In a study of 148 female therapists, it was found that counseling sexual violence survivors might trigger vicarious trauma, independent of the counselor's history (Schauben & Frazier, 1995).

If you are working in situations where you see people victimized by fires, rapes, battering, or other brutal events, it can be difficult to be unaffected by the stories you hear daily and not carry the graphic pictures with you. It is very common for therapists working with these populations and listening to the horrific descriptions to have spontaneous images appear unbidden, similar to the flashbacks experienced in post-traumatic stress. Nightmares, emotional numbing, and dissociative experiences may be part of the symptom package, as well as increased cynicism and disconnection from others. Studies find that newcomers in the caring professions are especially vulnerable to being overwhelmed by the realities of others because they haven't yet developed strong emotional boundaries (Skovholt & Ronnestad, 2001).

Vicarious traumatization is sometimes referred to as "compassion fatigue" (Figley, 2002) and seems to occur most in those providers who are most caring and empathetic (Figley, 1995). The most compassionate people burn out the most, with many experiencing bad dreams and other debilitating symptoms. Therapists who "care too much," those who show the most compassion and caring, are most likely to suffer from these symptoms because they hear stories about people they care about and can identify with.

Unlike a television show, where you can switch off the set or close your eyes when the images become too gruesome, you cannot do that when working with clients, and by being forced to listen, you become a witness to their catastrophic events. It hurts because you care for your patients, and it hurts because it causes feelings of vulnerability, helplessness, and anger in you, particularly if you are a compassionate and sensitive therapist. The trauma may also bring to the surface some of your own issues, including the fact that what happened to them could happen to you.

Empathy is a double-edged sword. On the one hand, it is the very ability to feel what your client is feeling that makes you effective; on the other hand, if you feel too much, you can become overwhelmed yourself. If you work with trauma patients, you need to learn to balance objectivity and empathy. Christina Maslach (1982) calls this "detached concern," that ideal blend of compassion and detachment where you have a more sensitive understanding of what your client is going through without being blinded by your feelings. It is being emotionally involved, while simultaneously maintaining a professional distance. This is, in many instances, easier said than done. How do you shut off the feelings in you while your client talks about the loss of her only son? Or when a woman who has been coming to your office week after week for years is dealing with the ravaging effects of cancer? Or how do you watch the disintegration of a client you have come to care for, without falling apart yourself or shutting down?

Some situations may bring on painful feelings more than others do, especially if your life circumstances mirror the client's. "I just lost it," Marion reported when the man she was treating brought pictures of his very ill infant grandson. She could happily identify with him throughout his daughter's pregnancy, particularly because her own daughter was expecting a child. When she saw the pictures, she was devastated. That could have been her grandchild.

Compassion fatigue is an extreme form of burnout, and the same suggestions that were given in Chapter 15 apply here, only more so. If you are suffering from symptoms of post-traumatic stress or from emotional fatigue, are withdrawing, or want to avoid your patients altogether, view these as signs of burnout and as a cue to take care of yourself. If you find the work emotionally draining and are carrying the trauma with you, recognize that you are human, and remind yourself that the providers most likely to experience compassion fatigue are those who are most compassionate. Don't take your emotions as a form of weakness. Understand that you have been traumatized, and do the same things for yourself that you would do for your clients.

Although most of the time you're only *listening* to stories of traumatic happenings, sometimes you may *experience* those in therapy. Probably the most stressful event that I witnessed as a psychotherapist occurred many years ago when I was leading an inpatient group, and one of the members tried to jump out a glass window. It was the first—and, I hope, the last—time that I or anyone else in that room saw someone try to kill himself right in front of our eyes. Luckily, other staff members and patients tackled him and prevented his suicide (later on, after he was transferred to a safer environment, he thanked us for saving his life). All of us had just observed a near tragedy and experienced similar symptoms following this event, for the rest of that day and for days afterward. As a group, we processed what happened and expressed our strong emotions. We talked together and cried together and tried to work through our feelings together. I recall going through the scene over and over in my mind and reliving the ordeal for days afterward. Today, I know that what I experienced were symptoms of post-traumatic stress, even though at that time this was not an official diagnosis.

Fortunately for me, I was able to talk about this incident with my co-workers because many of us had gone through it together. However, many therapists are not always able to do so if the trauma is not such a "public" one. Some clinicians allow their pride, as well as confidentiality issues, to get in the way of sharing their feelings with their peers. I have devoted a chapter each to the importance of speaking to your colleagues and getting some personal therapy. Nowhere are these more relevant than when you are having symptoms of compassion fatigue. You need a place to process your emotions and get the necessary distance from them.

I shared the story of the man who attempted to jump out the window with Jim, a male therapist who dealt directly with violent clients as part of his job. Jim worked in a setting where he not only had to interact with explosive patients every day, he frequently needed to break up fights, putting himself at risk. Jim didn't think any of the symptoms he was experiencing—apathy, lack of enthusiasm for his job, and general malaise—had anything to do with the conditions of his work. After all, he was a big, sturdy, macho guy, and, furthermore, he had been to war and had experienced situations much worse than the one he was in now. He said that my sharing with him that I had cried together with my clients allowed him to recognize that the trauma of witnessing violence daily does get through, in spite of solid, intact defenses. It gave him permission to discharge his emotions—to cry about the incidents, talk about them, and do whatever else we tell our clients to do to deal with their ordeals. For many clinicians, particularly men who are taught to be strong and silent, admitting to these feelings of vulnerability may be perceived as a sign of weakness. If you find yourself becoming withdrawn, bored, and detached from your work, pay attention to whether this may be a form of compassion fatigue, and talk about what you are going through with a colleague or a therapist.

Learn To Deal with Negative Countertransference

Although compassion fatigue may occur because you "care *too much*" for your clients, you may be experiencing just the opposite; you may have strong *negative* feelings for them and find a few people so extremely stressful that you want to avoid them altogether, as Lisa did. Although there are hazards in getting *too* close to your patients, there are pitfalls in wanting to get as far away from them as possible, unless, of course, they are a danger to your safety.

If you are having less than positive reactions to your clients, you are not alone. In a large and rather disturbing national survey of hundreds of psychologists, 80% of the respondents reported some rather intense and unsettling feelings about those they treat (Pope & Tabachnick, 1993). Most significant are the findings reflecting therapists' anger, hate, and fear toward their clients in relation to personal boundaries.

Even though most of the people you see may elicit very positive feelings in you, only one or two troublesome patients can be major annoyances. In fact, "work with difficult clients (e.g., suicidal, borderline traits)" was the most frequently endorsed item by clinicians (72%) as a work factor causing stress (Sherman & Thelen, 1998). Most practitioners I surveyed also listed difficult clients as more than mere nuisances. Following are a few responses about what were some of the most significant stresses of being a therapist:

"Probably the most stressful have involved my own safety, for example, working with angry, volatile clients with a history of violence."

"Working with people who are extremely difficult, hostile, or nasty. Sometimes these people might qualify for a borderline personality diagnosis, but sometimes not."

"Dealing with personality disorders"

"Homicidal, suicidal, or psychotic clients"

"I worry about my personal safety with some clients."

Although the definition of a difficult client will vary for different people, studies have found some common characteristics and behaviors of clients that make these people very stressful for clinicians to work with (Kottler, 1992; Robbins, Beck, Mueller, & Mizener, 1988). The list includes clients who have hidden agendas, ignore boundaries, refuse responsibility, have poor impulse control, are actively suicidal, bring up your unresolved issues, or remind you of someone from the past. Clients with physiological disorders, such as a head injury or those who are literal and concrete, can also evoke intense feelings.

If you are experiencing a negative reaction to someone you are working with, try to discover what is behind it so that it does not interfere with your treatment of that person. Studies show not only that negative countertransference is related to poor working alliances (Ligiero & Gelso, 2002) but that therapists are less inclined to want to treat people they don't like, even when these individuals are in greater need for psychotherapy (Lehman & Salovey, 1990).

How many of your feelings have to do with you, and how many of them are a reaction to what the client is doing? I have already stressed the importance of undergoing personal therapy as a way of knowing yourself and keeping your instrument clean. When you find yourself having a strong countertransference to a particular patient, talk it over with another colleague if you are not seeing a therapist. I call this "checking out your instrument." If the client is eliciting intense feelings in you because he or she acts like your boss, ex-spouse, or parent, this will help you recognize that and correct your own biases. However, if your patient is indeed "difficult" and his or her behavior is evoking a negative reaction in you, it is important to maintain a healthy distance for your sake, as well as for his or hers, or you'll end up being countertherapeutic. For more on the subject, I suggest Jeffrey Kottler's book *Compassionate Therapy: Working with Difficult Clients* (1992).

Don't Work with Clients Who Intimidate You

If personal safety is an issue, don't work with clients who threaten you: Screen them out and avoid them as much as possible. Only you know your emotional and physical limits, and only you can decide if a client is dangerous to you. Don't be "brave" like Jim and put yourself at risk. Pay attention to your body's signals, and refuse to see anyone who intimidates you in any way. Remember, there are no "objective" criteria that tell you that your client is dangerous. After numerous studies on the subject, it is widely accepted that future violent behavior cannot be predicted with great accuracy (Stromberg, Schneider, & Joondeph, 1993).

If you are unwittingly put into a situation where you fear bodily harm from a patient, attempt to diffuse the anger as much as possible, and then stop working with the person. As in other sticky circumstances requiring clinical judgment, discuss with a colleague, a supervisor, or a therapist the best way to do that. Your physical safety is paramount, and you will need to do whatever you can to keep yourself protected. In some rare cases, keeping a healthy distance may mean moving to another state and even into another profession, as one therapist did after being stalked.

Unfortunately, being threatened, harassed, or attacked by a patient is becoming more common and is likely to occur at some point in a mental health professional's work (Tishler, Gordon, & Landry-Meyer, 2000). If you are working with aggressive clients, the authors provide guidelines on creating a healthy distance when dealing with violent or potentially violent patients.

Even if your physical being isn't at risk, you don't need to treat individuals who are rude, demeaning, or disrespectful. Lottie, a marriage counselor, received a call one evening from an irate husband. He yelled at her, cursed her, and blamed her for the state of his marriage. She listened to his verbal barrage for a long time, not saying anything and getting angrier by the minute. The next day, the man came in for his regular session and barely mentioned the phone call. When Lottie told him that his behavior the previous evening was rude and inappropriate and that she expected an apology, he replied, "But you're a therapist. Your job is to listen and be understanding." Unfortunately, many counselors feel the same way as well. As therapists, they feel that they are supposed to be unconditionally accepting, be empathetic, and listen as their clients "express their anger." You would not take verbal abuse from anyone else, and you do not need to tolerate it from your clients either. You are not a punching bag, and you should demand the same kind of respect from the people you treat that you would from anyone else.

A psychotherapeutic relationship is one of mutual respect and trust, and if a client disrespects you and violates that trust, it is important to let him or her know that. Jerry, a psychologist, felt cheated by his patient, who refused to pay his bills after treatment was completed, despite repeated calls. When the client called months later for an appointment, Jerry told him that a therapy relationship was one of trust, and he could not work with someone who had deliberately taken advantage of him. If you have been taught that a therapist should always be accepting of a client's behavior, remind yourself that psychotherapy is based on *mutual* respect and trust, and that you cannot have an honest collaboration with someone who willfully abuses that bond. You cannot be therapeutic if you have strong negative feelings toward the person you are counseling. Of course, only you know what your limits are and how much of the client's actions are fodder for therapy and when they cross the line into unacceptable behavior. You will, of course, also want to use your judgment and consult with a colleague or a supervisor to decide when it is appropriate to confront the person and when it may be wiser not to—for example, if you are dealing with a dangerous or vindictive individual.

Use Cognitive Tools To Create a Healthy Distance

Many of the suggestions so far have been about providing a healthy *physical* distance when you have negative reactions—either by screening clients up front or removing yourself afterward. What do you do when you are in a situation where you have to work with clients for whom you have an intense dislike? How can you minimize these feelings so that they do not interfere with your well-being or that of the person you are treating? If, after assessing the situation, you recognize that the person is indeed being "difficult," pay attention to any negative thoughts you have that may be intensifying the situation, and then try to change them.

Ed, a compassionate, sensitive therapist, says this: "My strategy for dealing with this is to try to avoid nasty people—or at least, if I have to, to continually remind myself this is their problem, it is not a reflection of who I am or my skills." Ed is essentially focusing on the process of the interaction and not on the content, which helps put a healthy therapeutic space between him and his clients. Other clinicians have also mentioned making statements to themselves that help diffuse the negative feelings they have toward their clients: "He doesn't know how to relate to others—that's why he's here," or "If I can just see some of the fear beneath the outburst, I can keep my cool and be therapeutic," or "Let me pay attention to exactly what she's doing. Let me focus on the process. What behaviors is he or she specifically engaging in to get me so agitated?"

If you are feeling particularly frustrated or irritated, some self-statements for controlling anger (Novaco, 1975) can help you calm down and become more empathetic. Repeating to yourself, "There's no point in getting mad"; "For him to act like this, he must be really unhappy"; or, my personal favorite, "I can't expect people to act the way I want them too" can be very useful. Just acknowledging to yourself that the client is operating under different rules than you would like aids in creating some therapeutic distance. So can a reminder that the client—not you—has to live with the consequences of his or her behavior.

Nina, a social worker employed at an agency where at times she is forced to work with psychopaths and what she terms "evil" people, uses a "protection mantra": "I literally project an invisible shield in my solar plexus to ward off negative vibes, especially when I'm working with a very negative population." She adds, "There have been times when I have felt emotionally stabbed, and the protection mantra served as a detachment."

A healthy distance between you and your clients is one that enables you to function optimally, with consequent benefits for them. If you are either too close because you care too much, or too far because you care too little, it can be countertherapeutic. Recognize the hazards of dealing with emotionally laden material day in and day out. You can prevent your patients' crises from becoming yours when you maintain a historical perspective and focus on the therapeutic process. Having a sense of humor and defining clear boundaries also help you keep a safe distance.

Learn to recognize the symptoms of "caring too much" so that you can avoid vicarious traumatization. Also pay attention to "caring too little." When you want to remove yourself from clients, check out your "instrument" and see how much of your feelings have to do with your issues and how much with theirs. For therapy to be effective, you need an atmosphere of mutual respect and trust. If you are unable to have these feelings for your clients—and vice versa—keep a healthy physical distance. Try to avoid working with people when these elements aren't present, particularly if you feel threatened or intimidated, rather than attempting to "tough it out." If you cannot physically remove yourself from the situation, use cognitive techniques to maintain a healthy emotional distance for you.

Self-Assessment

Am I showing any of these signs of "caring too much"?

_____ Becoming overinvolved with my clients' problems

_____ Overidentifying with clients

_____ Working harder than the client

_____ Showing indications of compassion fatigue or secondary trauma, for example, emotional numbing, nightmares, shutting down, unable to switch off, or other symptoms

_____ (Other) ____

If yes, which of these would work for me in creating a healthy emotional distance?

_____ Recognizing the hazards of being a therapist

_____ Not allowing my clients' crises to become mine by keeping a historical perspective

_____ Paying attention to my clients' processes

_____ Setting more boundaries with clients

_____ Using humor

_____ Talking to a colleague, a supervisor, or a therapist

_____ (Other) ____

Am I showing signs of "caring too little"?

_____ Feeling helpless or frustrated with a client

_____ Feeling bored or impatient with a client

_____ Feeling angry or agitated with a client

_____ Speaking about a client in disrespectful terms

_____ Dreading to see a particular client and wanting to avoid him or her

_____ (Other) ____

What are some strategies to help me diffuse these negative feelings?

_____ Trying to understand my reactions by talking to a colleague, a supervisor, or a therapist

_____ Creating a physical distance when my physical or emotional safety is compromised

_____ Using cognitive tools to create a healthy distance

_____ (Other) ____

CHAPTER 21

Learn To Deal with Uncertainty

Peace is not needing to know what will happen next.
—Anonymous

Uncertainty is part and parcel of being a therapist, and learning to deal with this on a daily basis is essential to your happiness and well-being. The very nature of psychotherapy is ambiguous, and looking for the "right" way to do it can, in and of itself, be frustrating. Similarly, there is no predictability in outcome, and despite your best interventions, your clients do not always respond as you would like them to. The vagueness of the therapy task and, in many instances, the lack of measurable, quantifiable results also make for stress. In addition to the emotional insecurities that stem from being a therapist, there are frequently financial ones as well, especially for professionals in private practice, particularly for beginning therapists but not limited to those. The emotional and economic unpredictability inherent in being a psychotherapist can add to your stress level, and learning to ride the waves is important for you. In this chapter, I will discuss the ways to deal with the emotional uncertainty, as well as with business fluctuations if you work for yourself.

Challenge Beliefs That Lead to Insecurity

If you are experiencing feelings of unsettledness, take a look at the underlying thoughts that may be contributing to them. In Chapter 19, I touched on some of these mind-sets that are self-defeating and only add to your distress, for example, "I should be all things to all people." The overresponsibility trap, feeling overly accountable for your clients' progress, is certainly one that can lead to burnout. Having unrealistic expectations is another one, and I discussed the value of setting realistic goals; keeping a time perspective; focusing on the process, rather than on the outcome of therapy; and not taking what happens personally as antidotes to the type of thinking you indulge in when you get into the overresponsibility trap.

Edelwich and Brodsky (1980) list a few other assumptions that bring on stress, such as the idea that it is a dire necessity for a clinician to be loved and appreciated by every client or to always enjoy the favor of supervisors. They suggest applying rational-emotive therapy to these thoughts and challenging them. Other common beliefs that can lead to insecurity are that a person should become very upset over clients' problems or failings and that it is awful or catastrophic when clients (or systems) do not behave as you'd like them to. If you are engaging in that type of thinking, reread parts of the last chapter, and don't allow your patients' crises to become your own. If you feel particularly agitated after a session, write down *exactly* what you have been telling yourself and learn to challenge your thoughts.

One piece of research-tested advice for mental health practitioners is to avoid self-blame and wishful thinking (Norcross, 2000). These two strategies are associated with ineffective self-care—what *not* to do. When clinicians berate themselves and focus on what they *cannot* do, they increase their distress and reduce problem solving. Their energies go into blaming and wishing, rather than into acting. If you are chastising yourself for your client's actions ("I should have . . .") or if you concentrate on what you cannot do or wish that things were different ("If only . . ."), see how you can change these negative thoughts into more constructive and realistic ones.

Don't View Uncertainty as a Measure of Your Competency

One belief that causes many therapists anxiety has to do with unrealistic expectations about what they should know or be able to handle. A corollary to the assumption "I should know everything" (and derivations thereof) is "I must be totally competent and successful to be worthwhile." Seeing this thought in black and white highlights its absurdity, yet many practitioners start to doubt their adequacy when they feel like they are operating in the dark. This has been termed the "imposter phenomenon" (Clance & Imes, 1978) and is particularly acute for female psychology graduate students and beginners in other professions where they are *expected* to know things but are still learning. They may have the title but not the necessary skills. Consequently, they feel like imposters. Everyone presumes they are experts, yet they know they are novices. Many graduate students and therapists are afraid to express these feelings, particularly to their supervisors, who evaluate them, or to their peers, with whom they are in direct competition. They are afraid they will be seen as stupid, inadequate, lacking, or any combination of these.

I mentioned earlier that it takes a long time to develop feelings of confidence and competency as a clinician, although many therapists think they should be able to conduct therapy effortlessly right away. When they don't, they berate themselves and start questioning their abilities.

Having supervised many students and therapists who have shared these feelings with me, I tell them I am much more concerned about students who don't have "imposter" feelings—those who "know it all" right away. Their arrogance, overconfidence, and black-and-white thinking about complex and ambiguous situations frighten me, as they should. Studies on therapists' competence suggest that for optimal development to occur, practitioners need to continuously reflect upon their experiences and resist premature closure. The closing off of feedback, with little time taken to process or learn from mistakes, leads to emotional stagnation (Ronnestad & Skovholt, 2001; Skovholt & Ronnestad, 2001).

If you feel like an imposter or a phony, as much as possible, get good solid training and have a firm theoretical framework to work from. The more you learn something, the more confidant you will feel about what you are doing. Don't be afraid to ask questions and get the structure and the foundation you need to build on. With that being said, it is important to recognize that proper training takes time—and practice—and more time and more practice. Just mere repetition is not enough. The same studies show that processing and learning from experience are crucial to developing a high level of competence.

Learning to do therapy is like learning a foreign language or mastering any new skill. Expertise doesn't come right away. You cannot learn to speak a new language fluently just by reading about it. You have to hear it *daily* and you have to practice it *often*. It may feel awkward at first, and it may not always come naturally to you. However, only with much time and practice—and falling flat on your face often—can you start to feel comfortable with it. From the literature on the nature of expertise, we know that it takes hundreds and hundreds of hours to become skilled in conducting complex tasks such as psychotherapy (Chi, Glaser, & Farr, 1988) and that optimal professional development is a long, slow, and erratic process (Skovholt & Ronnestad, 2001).

Many years ago, I was introduced to the four stages of learning that I have found to be useful to students and clients when they start doubting themselves about their competencies. Think of any skill that you now do effortlessly—say, driving. Go back to the time before you learned to drive a car. You may have seen someone behind the wheel and thought, "That looks easy." The first stage of learning is *unconscious incompetence*—you don't even know what you don't know. Then you get in the driver's seat and have no idea what to do. Now you *really* feel stupid! That is the second stage—*conscious incompetence.* You take some driving lessons and keep at it until you can maneuver the car, but you still have to very consciously tell yourself: "brake," "press the gas pedal," "change signals," and so on. That's the third stage of *conscious competence.* You have learned the skill, but it's not automatic yet. Only after a great deal of practice do you get to the fourth stage of *unconscious competence,* where you get behind the wheel and drive effortlessly without thinking about it. Most abilities require these four steps before you master them. Unfortunately, many people want to get from stage 1 to stage 4 immediately. It is important to remember that the two phases in-between—conscious incompetence and conscious competence—are often *very* uncomfortable, particularly stage 2.

The research on practitioner development (Skovholt & Ronnestad, 2001) is in line with the four stages of learning. Novices rely on external expertise, whereas senior therapists depend on internal knowledge. Not surprisingly, beginners experience much more stress.

Remind yourself of these four steps of learning while you are acquiring knowledge in the art of therapy. Don't be scared or start to doubt yourself, and teach yourself to take things slowly and with much patience. Whether you are trying to become proficient in a therapy approach with a day workshop or a semester course, repeat to yourself that it takes a great deal of time and practice before the pieces fall into place and the task becomes more simple.

It is much easier to learn to speak a new language or drive a car than it is to conduct therapy because there is, in fact, a "correct" way to drive a car, speak a language, operate a computer, or perform any other objective skill. Part of the discomfort with performing therapy is that there is usually no absolutely "right" way to do it. Even approaches that are taught in a step-by-step fashion require judgment, sensitivity, and flexibility in how and when to use them because you're working with people and not machines.

As Dr. Lorna Smith Benjamin (2001), a psychologist, writes in her personal and professional reflections about psychodynamic therapy: "I was uncomfortable with the vagueness of it all. I quickly learned that it was a sign of rigidity (probably obsessive-compulsive disorder) to expect clearer thinking and a better understanding of how therapy was supposed to work. I figured out that to learn dynamically oriented therapy, one was supposed to hang around people who claimed to know and try to do what one imagined they did. Therapy was a highly private matter, so observing a senior clinician doing therapy was out of the question" (p. 21).

As much as possible, get concrete, specific feedback and supervision, as well as structured training, to deal with uncomfortable feelings when learning new skills. Observe, do, practice—keep doing it and learn from your mistakes. However, remind yourself to be patient and that uncertainty is part of the learning process and not a measure of your competency.

Don't Be Needy, Don't Be Greedy

In addition to emotional unsettledness, financial uncertainty is another hazard for some therapists (Kramen-Kahn & Hansen, 1998). If you are working for yourself, the ebb and flow of practice, the inconsistency, with some weeks full and others empty, can become a stressor. The economic instability, particularly during slow times, can be as worrisome as some of the psychological vagueness of a psychotherapy practice. Learn to deal with these monetary insecurities for your sake and for that of your clients. Don't be needy and don't be greedy or you'll end up making wrong decisions, holding on to patients longer than you have to, for your needs rather than for theirs. Set up your life so that you don't have to be either needy or greedy. In previous chapters I outlined how to manage your external world to relieve financial stress—by cutting costs, lowering your overhead, and simplifying your life as much as possible to provide yourself with the freedom to pursue doing what you love. In this chapter, I will elaborate on how to change your inner environment to match your outer one.

First of all, operate from a position of confidence and faith. When your behavior is ruled by fear and doubt, you will make foolhardy choices. Many new therapists, in their insecurity, work long hours, join dysfunctional panels, accept patients whom they find difficult to work with, and put up with many conditions that are neither personally nor professionally good for them because they feel desperate. In hindsight, they regret those decisions. This is akin to getting married to the first person who is interested because you are afraid there will be nobody else.

A clinging attitude will attract clients for the wrong reasons. Co-dependent and people-pleasing patients will want to come to take care of their therapists. They may sense the counselor's business insecurities and want to rescue him or her, forgetting that psychotherapy is for *their* needs and not for those of the person who is treating them. Conversely, they may withdraw altogether because they perceive that the therapist's insistence on extra sessions is more for his or her benefit than for theirs. "I decided to stop going to my analyst," a man told me. "He reminds me of my broker, who keeps suggesting investments because of the commissions he makes." If you find yourself accepting clients you would not normally see or holding on to them longer than necessary, remind yourself of this basic rule: *The patient's needs come first.* Whatever decisions you make in therapy, do them for the welfare of your client and not to ease your own fears.

George Weinberg (1984), in his advice to therapists, states, "I have always been fascinated by the degree to which patients are able to infer the therapist's attitude about money. How badly does the therapist need it? Does he see the patient primarily as a source of income?" (p. 38). He continues, "I advise all beginning therapists to try to make some money out of something besides their practice, so that they won't communicate this neediness" (p. 39).

In addition to operating from a position of confidence, learn to let go. As a psychiatrist wrote in her advice to new therapists: "Don't chase patients, but do call them back promptly and also call them when you are concerned about them between appointments." As you can see, letting go doesn't mean neglecting the people you treat or not showing concern about them. Learn to release your clients gracefully, much like a parent with a child. It is their time and money, and, except in those situations where it's clearly counterindicated (e.g., they are still suicidal etc.), it is important to let them go willingly, leaving the door open for the future, and without a guilt trip! Weinberg (1984) reports a curious phenomenon that occurs once a therapist feels more secure and learns to let go: The referrals start coming from everywhere.

Check to see if you are carrying any self-limiting beliefs that may be contributing to your economic insecurity, such as, "You need to work evenings and weekends to survive in private practice," "You can't make a living unless you join HMO panels," and other similar messages of doom and gloom that may be adding to your fears. In particular, don't engage in catastrophic thinking when your caseload dwindles ("I'll never get another referral again"). At those times, remind yourself of the natural fluctuations—the rhythm—of practice, and enjoy the slow times instead of getting alarmed.

Other beliefs that may contribute to your feelings of economic unsettledness might have to do with your attitudes about receiving compensation for your services. I alluded to some of these in Chapter 12. Many therapists have a complicated relationship with money, which creates a great deal of guilt and conflict for them (Herron & Welt, 1992). As Kottler (1993) says, "We cannot decide whether therapy is essentially a profession or a business" (p. 111). Consequently, they may undercharge, not collect, or engage in behaviors that keep them from receiving proper compensation for their services. If you feel financially insecure, see if any of these beliefs may be contributing to the situation: "I shouldn't be getting paid for doing something I like"; "I'm not really doing 'anything'"; "Therapists get paid too much"; or "I'm not in this for the money." If they are, remind yourself that you are providing a valuable service, and you need to be reimbursed for it.

Learn to change the negative self-talk to more positive, realistic thoughts. Think thoughts of abundance ("there's plenty to go around") and self-worth ("my security is me"). My good friend Jackie Bradley likes to say, "It's only money." This really helps one to gain perspective. A story that I heard and frequently tell others to help them put their economic worries into focus concerns a movie star whose jewelry was stolen. As she was sobbing over the loss, her co-star said to her, "Don't cry over anything that can't cry over you."

A therapist once told me that she is still looking for that magic number of clients in private practice—somewhere between too few and too many. I'm not sure what that figure would be. If it does seem too slow, use up the hours with other professional activities—writing that chapter, reading that book, or preparing that workshop. Or spend the time on personal pleasures—going to a museum, a movie, or a shopping mall.

If your practice gets *too* empty, ask yourself what is going on. Do you need to do more marketing? Should you be seeking other venues? Is there something you need to do or change? The blank spaces in your appointment book may also be your unconscious saying you need more breathing space and to free up hours for new pursuits. Megan, for example, found her caseload "magically" shrinking just as she was preparing to go to school, as if in response to her request to have time to attend classes. Pamela's numbers also went down, as if she was unconsciously making room in her schedule to take care of her new grandchild. Libby's patients dropped down to just the right amount, to adjust to her being on the road.

"What if 'the worst' happens? I know it's unlikely, but suppose, despite the normal ebb and flow of practice, my clients swindle down to *nothing?*" a therapist—I'll call her Laura—asked me. If, like Laura, you worry about the "worst-case scenario," tell yourself that you are an intelligent person with many resources, that you have a graduate degree, and that your specialty is helping people manage their lives. If you have more time on your schedule, use that opportunity to figure out how to thrive, instead of engaging in energy-draining rumination.

I am reminded of the story of a young man, a musician recently out of college, who was getting panicky because of the tight job market. He took the first job he found—selling calendars at the mall—to alleviate his anxiety while he was looking for "real" work. He hated every minute of it, and after a week or two he thought that he would die of boredom. He quit, knowing he had no alternative but to spend every spare minute looking for employment doing something he loved, instead of wasting his time at someplace "safe" until he could land a job. He then used all of his energy pounding the pavements to find work in his field. A few weeks later, he had made numerous contacts and was making money at several different places, utilizing his skills and talents—loving every minute of it and earning more than double what he did selling calendars.

If the "worst" happens, don't be alarmed and act out of fear, taking the first dependable thing you can find. Use your time and energy marketing yourself and looking for employment opportunities, instead of panicking and doing something you hate, whether it is seeing difficult clients, participating in crazy-making systems, or working unreasonable hours, just because these are "safe." Your security—monetary and otherwise—comes from you.

Self-Assessment

If you are experiencing feelings of insecurity as a therapist, see if any of the following may be adding to your stress. Check all that apply.

Do any of these contribute to my feelings of uncertainty?

_____ Feeling overly accountable for my clients' progress

_____ Having unrealistic expectations for myself or my clients

_____ Engaging in self-blame ("I should have . . .")

_____ Engaging in wishful thinking ("If only . . .")

_____ Viewing my uncertainty as a measure of my competency

_____ Feeling like an imposter

_____ (Other) ____

Which of the following strategies can I use to deal with those feelings?

_____ Looking at the underlying thoughts behind my insecurity and challenging them

_____ Getting good solid training, feedback, or supervision

_____ Understanding that uncertainty is part of the learning process, that expertise takes time, and that optimal practitioner development is long, slow, and erratic

_____ Learning from my mistakes

_____ (Other) ____

If you are in practice and experiencing feelings of financial insecurity, check if any of these beliefs or behaviors may be contributing to your stress.

Which of these may be contributing to my feelings of financial unsettledness?

_____ Feeling I need to be working evenings and weekends to survive in private practice

_____ Believing that I can't make a living unless I join HMO panels

_____ Working with people who make my life miserable or putting up with conditions that are not conducive to my personal or professional development

_____ Getting very anxious when my caseload dwindles

_____ Holding on to clients for my needs, rather than for theirs

_____ Undercharging, not collecting, or engaging in behaviors that keep me from receiving proper compensation for my services

_____ (Other) ____

Which of these strategies can help me deal with the feelings of financial unsettledness?

_____ Setting up my life so that I don't have to be needy or greedy

_____ Operating from a position of confidence and faith, rather than of fear and doubt

_____ Exploring my self-defeating behaviors about money and changing them

_____ Charging adequately for my services and ensuring that I receive proper compensation

_____ Learning to let go

_____ Reminding myself of the natural ebb and flow of practice

_____ Using the slow times for other activities

_____ (Other) ____

CHAPTER 22

Remember Your Calling

The purpose of calls is to summon adherents from their daily grinds to a new level of awareness, into a sacred frame of mind, into communion with that which is bigger than themselves.
—Gregg Levoy, *Callings*

I have talked at length about the emotional risks for clinicians of conducting therapy on a day-to-day basis. At times, you may get so focused on the stresses inherent in being a therapist that you may not see the transcending bigger picture. You have to tell yourself over and over why you are doing this work to begin with and appreciate the higher purpose of your calling—to look beyond the daily hassles of not enough time, conflicting demands, endless forms to fill out, unrealistic expectations, or other factors. In this chapter, I will elaborate on how to reap the rewards of your profession and go beyond some of the strains of practicing therapy.

Remind Yourself of the Higher Meaning of Your Work

It is sometimes so easy to get bogged down with details that you forget the deeper significance of your job. Ask yourself, "What is my purpose? What is my mission?" Your response to that question gives meaning to everything you do and transforms the other stuff. Ben, a therapist whose work primarily involves alleviating others' suffering, reminds himself, "I am a healer." He keeps this mantra, his aim in life, foremost in his mind, and it helps him navigate through the maze of insurance companies, paperwork, financial pressures, and some of the day-to-day hassles of the profession. He recognizes his mission. He's doing what he needs to do—what comes naturally to him and what he learned with many years of training. As Gregg Levoy (1997) says, "Even the highest calling entails the unremarkable tasks of licking stamps, stuffing envelopes, and tacking up flyers. It asks that we do our homework, sweep the front porch, sock away pennies, and knock on wood" (p. 279).

When you have defined your path, it gives value to everything you do and surmounts the hard work and frustration. Eliza is a counselor who helps people who have lost loved ones. She did not initially set out to do this type of work, but it gradually evolved following the death of her children. Knowing the devastating effects of grief, she chose as her goal alleviating the suffering of others who are mourning. Eliza puts in long hours. She conducts workshops, leads groups, consults, travels, and spends an enormous amount of time and energy pursuing her mission. She is one of the most loving, nurturing, compassionate, generous, and creative people I know and seems to run on unlimited fuel. She also has a unique way with arts and crafts and combines that with her grief work. Whenever she is complimented on her extraordinary achievements, she states simply, "This is what I do," not recognizing that what comes to her so naturally is truly a gift. Her work, rather than draining her, is nourishing. She is simply following her path: "This is what I do."

Marvin is another one of those remarkable healers. Following the loss of his son, he found his goal in helping other children. Marvin started out by volunteering one afternoon a week in a small, impoverished neighborhood by his church and gradually expanded that program until it became a flourishing community for little kids. Like Eliza, Marvin seems to have unlimited energy and generosity when he is doing pursuing his mission, and, like her, he shrugs off his achievements. For both Eliza and Marvin, there is almost no ego involved. They see the *meaning* in their work that *transcends* the daily frustrations.

When you see the "big picture" behind all you're doing, it puts things into perspective and makes many of the little inconveniences irrelevant. Meaning gives importance to all you do and provides energy, rather than saps it. The same task can be invigorating or draining, depending on the significance you attach to it. Studies have shown that when people saw their work as a socially useful calling, rather than as a job or a career, they worked more hours, missed less work, and derived greater satisfaction from life than did others doing similar work. It did not matter whether the job was a clerical or a professional job—it was how they viewed it that was important (Wrzesniewski, McCauley, Rozin, & Schwartz, 1997).

A man representing an agency calling for volunteers to go overseas to a conflicted region during a crisis said he was overwhelmed by the huge response he got. "When we wanted tourists and offered them great packages at luxury hotels, nobody came. When we asked for volunteers who would only have basic accommodations, everyone wants to come!" It is interesting that when people feel *needed,* when they see a higher *meaning* to what they are doing, they will do the same task, and the physical inconveniences do not seem to matter. It is as if the sense of purpose provides the energy and rises above the bodily needs. Why would people risk even their *safety* going to a dangerous region to do something they wouldn't do under normal conditions? People volunteer because of the opportunity to be of service, to do something bigger than themselves.

To have a sense of purpose makes even the intolerable bearable. Nowhere is the importance of meaning more beautifully illustrated than in Viktor Frankl's *Man's Search for Meaning* (1959). Frankl, a psychiatrist who spent many years in a concentration camp during the Second World War, writes that man's concern is not to gain pleasure or avoid pain but to see a meaning in his life. That sense seems to surmount some of the most difficult suffering, even under deplorable conditions.

Although Ben, Eliza, Marvin, and Dr. Frankl were able to articulate their purpose, which surpassed small and large physical stresses, you may not always be so sure of your path or calling. Some guidelines are suggested by Bill O'Hanlon (2001), a therapist who has written numerous books and who conducts workshops nationwide. Like Marvin and Eliza, Bill O'Hanlon puts a great deal of energy into spreading his ideas and shares them freely. Like them, he is very generous with his time and talents, using them to teach and help others. A friend attending his workshop described him as "almost humble; there's no ego involved." One gets the sense that he has a higher mission, and that his purpose rises above personal gratification. The following are some of the questions he proposes you ask yourself to help you define your own path: What is your life purpose? What are you uniquely suited to contribute? What are you called to do? What makes you feel alive when you're doing it? What makes you feel energized even though you have exerted yourself? What would you talk about if you had an hour of prime time? Where do you feel at home, as if you belong or were meant to be doing? What gets you angry so that you feel moved enough to change? These are a few of the thought-provoking questions to get you started in defining the higher intent in what you do. Notice that it is a combination of what you believe in, what you are drawn to, and what you do naturally.

Diane Sawyer (2002), talk show host and reporter, relates how, when she chose her life work, she was asked three things by her father: "What is it that you love? Where is the most adventurous place you could do it? And are you certain it will serve other people?" Nowadays, whenever people ask her for career advice, she puts the three questions to them. If they can answer the first two, and they're sure about the third, she tells them it will be like one of those global positioning satellites—to take the road ahead and love the ride. Ms. Sawyer, like others, is an example of someone who takes her own special interests and talents and uses them for a higher good.

Leila is a healer. She is actually a radiology technician and does mammograms. She is so good at her job that her patients don't even notice the procedure and have no discomfort whatsoever. "Everyone has a gift," she says when she's complimented. "This is mine." Leila, like others before her, sees her job as important and uses her abilities to contribute what she is most suited to do. Look at your own unique talents, interests, and hobbies, what comes to you naturally, and if you can combine these with the deeper purpose of your work, you will feel energized, instead of depleted. The research on flow, when time seems to be whizzing by, concludes that finding a purpose to your work is the key to eliminating boredom and finding what you do stimulating, exciting, and fun (Csikszentmihalyi, 1990).

Dr. Martin Seligman (2002) echoes these same themes in his studies on finding authentic happiness beyond the monetary pleasures. Having a sense of purpose by engaging in philanthrophic activities or leaving a legacy that outlives you—using your own signature strengths—is one of the basic principles for having lasting fulfillment. Dr. Martin Luther King Jr. is reported to have said that you do your best work when you are engaged in something that will outlast you. When you see the *meaning* in what you do, it moves you from your own isolated self into a connection with something bigger than you. There is no ego involved. Marvin, Eliza, and Leila were simply taking their special gifts and using them to contribute to a purpose larger than themselves.

Open Up the Spiritual Dimension of Your Work and Your Life

Spirituality is often a taboo word in psychological circles because many people associate it with organized religion. It has largely been neglected in the training of therapists (Brawer, Handal, Fabricatore, Roberts, & Wajda-Johnson, 2002), despite the extensive body of research touting its many physical and psychological benefits (Hill & Pargament, 2003; Miller & Thoresen, 2003; Powell, Shahabi, & Thoresen, 2003; Seeman, Dubin, & Seeman, 2003). Spirituality can be an orienting, motivating force, providing direction and purpose in life and helping to sustain people even in the midst of disturbing life events.

I am using spirituality here in the way that Bill O'Hanlon (2001) uses it, as anything that gives you the experience of the "bigger self" or moves you beyond the limited personality. It is essentially connecting from the personal to something more universal. As I listened to him at the workshop talk about the three Cs of spirituality—connection, compassion, and contribution—I thought to myself that psychotherapy is truly one of those professions where these components are built in. It is one of the most spiritual activities you can partake in because it connects you with others, it is a way of "feeling with" them and also of being of unselfish service. The therapy hour is sacred time, time to be treasured without the confines or intrusions of outside distractions or interferences. It is holy in the sense that you are observing another human being share his or her soul. You are watching in wonder and participating in the unfolding of a life, with the same awe you'd experience in watching a child grow and develop. Psychotherapy utilizes the best of you and thus brings on the satisfactions inherent in the nature of your work. When you incorporate spirituality into your practice, you are focusing on the connection and the compassion in relating to another person and in contributing to his or her mental health.

To the three Cs of spirituality, I would like to add a fourth one—commitment—looking beyond the immediate rewards, being there for the long haul, and immersing yourself fully in the task at hand. In fact, the passionately committed therapists are those who are energized and invigorated by their work, rather than drained by it (Dlugos & Friedlander, 2001). A passionate commitment to their job reflects a passionate commitment in other areas as well. Energy is usually there for activities to which you are fully engaged, whereas doing something halfheartedly only leaves you feeling tired and depleted. A commitment to a calling is in some ways not that different from a commitment to a spouse, a child, or a friend whom you love very much or with whom you share a common goal. Even though it may be difficult at times, there is a higher purpose to it, allowing you to hang on through the ups and downs. Like other relationships, you may need to recommit from time to time to help you persevere. Every calling has mundane tasks associated with it and involves giving time and energy to seemingly minor and trivial tasks. The long-term purpose helps you rise above the boring and the mundane.

When you bring spirituality into your work or your life, it can transcend you and move you beyond the problem at hand. I was halfway finished writing this book when September 11 happened. Completing the manuscript suddenly became meaningless. How could I even write about being a happy therapist when the world had changed? Could one even be a happy person in these times? How could I bring up something so petty—even frivolous—in view of what was happening all over the world? I left the manuscript on the shelf—literally—and let it collect dust. I had signed up for O'Hanlon's workshop on therapy and spirituality before any of the terrible events occurred and attended it simply because I had already made arrangements. During the conference, he asked us to visualize a spiritual moment or a time when we had felt free, flowing, alive, and energetic and to recreate the experience. Then we were to bring that sense of spirituality to any situation we were currently feeling stuck in now or for the future. I immediately flashed on to my own "flow," when I'm writing, and can just feel the energy coming on. I pictured myself completing the book and was able to go beyond my own prison to a place of meaning and hope.

When you reach into something larger than you and feel that you are contributing, it moves you outside of yourself, past your stuck point. What are some ways of connecting to that something "beyond"? I talked about a few of these in previous chapters. Certainly, meditation, journal writing, prayer, and even spending time by yourself can get you most in touch with that deep voice within you and move you outside of yourself. Pay attention to your dreams, and listen to what they are saying to you. Develop your inner life through art, beauty, music, and other manners of soul nourishment.

Another venue that gets you "beyond" is nature. It is no wonder that so many people go to the mountains or the ocean or look at the stars to connect with something larger than themselves. Or you can carry nature indoors, by bringing plants into your home or office. Being with loved ones, with friends, and with the general community also reminds you that there is something greater than yourself.

You undoubtedly know of countless ways to enhance the spiritual aspects of your work. Connecting and compassion are the very essence of what you do as a therapist, and keeping these spiritual realms in the foreground—and not in the background—makes being a psychotherapist one of the most inherently rewarding professions. Directly contributing to another person's well-being, alleviating his or her distress, forces you outside of yourself and helps you transcend the daily grind of the job.

Appreciate the Rewards of Being a Therapist

As a therapist, you are privileged to have people share with you and trust you with their innermost thoughts and feelings. You are—as Yalom (2002) beautifully puts it—"cradlers of secrets." You have the good fortune to be privy to your clients' lives and to participate in their joys and sorrows. Psychotherapy is a life-changing profession, and to be able to be directly involved in helping others grow is one of the biggest satisfactions of the job.

Psychology was founded on the betterment of human welfare and on promoting social justice. The preamble to APA's first ethics code (1953), a code written in the aftermath of the Nazi holocaust, states that "the worth of a profession is measured by its contribution to the welfare of man." As a therapist, you are part of a very meaningful field, in which you can directly contribute and participate in others' well-being. Remind yourself of the value of your work and what a gift it is to be a witness to changes occurring daily within the sacred places of the therapy room. As a therapist, you are offering an oasis of calm, a sanctuary for people to bare and explore their psyches. "Everyone needs a place to cry," a wise woman once said. You are indeed fortunate to provide that place, a safe haven for secrets, tears, fears, and fantasies, a space where small and large miracles can happen daily.

It is not only your clients who are changed by psychotherapy. Clinicians tend to personally benefit from their work. In a study by Radeke and Mahoney (2000), therapists have said that their work has had a tremendous personal effect on them. It has made them more self-aware and wiser, has increased their psychological development and their capacity to enjoy life, and has felt like a spiritual service. As Norcross (2000) states, most practitioners feel enriched and privileged to be conducting therapy, and the work brings "relief, joy, meaning, growth, vitality, excitement, and genuine engagement, both for our patients and for us" (pp. 712–713).

As most of the colleagues I have surveyed have said in one form or other, working with other people and seeing them change is one of the most rewarding aspects of the therapy profession. Remember your calling—take your passions, interests, and talents and use them for a higher good. Most clinicians do just that. They love what they are doing and try to remind themselves why they are engaged in their work. They are also quick to point out that unless you have a deep and abiding interest in it, don't do it, or, as my good friend Larry Brock, a retired psychologist, likes to say, "Go to plumbing school!"

Self-Assessment

What is the higher meaning of my work?

How can I continually keep that purpose in the forefront when I am experiencing minor and major frustrations?

What are some ways I can enhance the spiritual aspects of my life and work?

What, for me, are the rewards of being a therapist?

References

Ackerley, G., Burnell, J., Holder, D., & Kurdek, L. (1988). Burnout among licensed psychologists. *Professional Psychology: Research and Practice, 19,* 624–631.

Ackerman, D. (1999). *Deep play.* New York: Random House.

Ackley, D. (1997). *Breaking free of managed care.* New York: Guilford.

Amabile, T. (1985). Motivation and creativity: Effects of motivational orientation on creative writing. *Journal of Personality and Social Psychology, 48,* 393–399.

American Psychological Association. (1953). *Ethical standards for psychologists: A summary of ethical principles.* Washington, DC: Author.

American Psychological Association. (2002). Ethical principles of psychologists and code of conduct. *American Psychologist, 57,* 1060–1073.

American Psychological Association Practice Directorate. (1994, July/August). *APA member focus groups on the health care environment: A summary report.* Washington, DC: Author.

Arthur, G., Brende, J., & Quiroz, S. (2003). Violence: Incidence and frequency of physical and psychological assaults affecting mental health providers in Georgia. *Journal of General Psychology, 130,* 22–45.

Bardwick, J. (1988). *The plateauing trap.* New York: Bantam.

Barnett, J. (2003). APA's revised ethics code: Implications for professional practice. *The Register Report, 29,* 10–11.

Barnett, J., & Hillard, D. (2001). Psychologist distress and impairment: The availability, nature, and use of colleague assistance programs for psychologists. *Professional Psychology: Research and Practice, 32,* 205–210.

Barnett, R., & Hyde, J. (2001). Women, men, work, and family: An expansionist theory. *American Psychologist, 56,* 781–796.

Beattie, M. (1987). *Codependent no more.* New York: Harper.

Beck, M. (2001). *Finding your own North Star.* New York: Crown.

Benjamin, L. (2001). A developmental history of a believer in history. In M. Goldfried (Ed.), *How therapists change.* Washington, DC: American Psychological Association.

Bohart, A. (2001). The evolution of an integrative experiential therapist. In M. Goldfried (Ed.), *How therapists change.* Washington, DC: American Psychological Association.

Bolton, L., Bolton, L., & Adams, A. (2002). *Time management: Get organized and accomplish more in less time.* Avon, MA: Adams Media Group.

Bonebright, C., Clay, D., & Ankenmann, R. (2000). The relationship of workaholism with work–life conflict, life satisfaction and purpose in life. *Journal of Counseling Psychology, 47,* 469–477.

Bory, D., & Pope, K. (1989). Dual relationships between therapist and client: A national study of psychologists, psychiatrists and social workers. *Professional Psychology: Research and Practice, 20,* 283–293.

Brady, J., Norcross, J., & Guy, J. (1995). Managing your own distress: Lessons from psychotherapists healing themselves. In L. VandeCreek, S. Knapp & T. Jackson (Eds.), *Innovations in clinical practice.* Sarasota, FL: Professional Resource Press.

Brawer, P., Handal, P., Fabricatore, A., Roberts, R., & Wajda-Johnston, V. (2002). Training and education in religion/spirituality within APA-accredited clinical psychology. *Professional Psychology: Research and Practice, 33,* 203–206.

Brown, L. (1997). The private practice of subversion. *American Psychologist, 52,* 449–462.

Burns, D. (1980, November). The perfectionist's script for self-defeat. *Psychology Today,* 34–52.

Buunk, B., & Verhoeven, K. (1991). Companionship and support at work: A microanalysis of the stress-reducing features of social interaction. *Basic and Applied Social Psychology, 12,* 243–258.

Byrne, A., & Byrne, D. (1993). The effect of exercise on depression, anxiety and other mood states: A review. *Journal of Psychosomatic Research, 376,* 565–574.

Cameron, J. (1992). *The artist's way.* New York: Jeremy P. Tarcher.

Campbell, C., & Gordon, M. (2003). Acknowledging the inevitable: Understanding multiple relationships in rural practice. *Professional Psychology: Research and Practice, 34,* 430–434.

Cherniss, C. (1995). *Beyond burnout.* New York: Brunner-Routledge.

Chi, M., Glaser, R., & Farr, M. (Eds.). (1988). *The nature of expertise.* Hillsdale, NJ: Erlbaum.

Clance, P., & Imes, S. (1978). The imposter phenomenon in high achieving women: Dynamics and therapeutic intervention. *Psychotherapy: Theory, Research and Practice, 15,* 241–247.

Coombs, R., & Fawzy, F. (1986). The impaired-physician syndrome: A developmental perspective. In C. Scott & J. Hawk (Eds.), *Heal thyself: The health of health care professionals.* New York: Brunner-Mazel.

Corder, B., & Whiteside, R. (1996). A survey of psychologists' safety issues and concerns. *American Journal of Forensic Psychology, 14,* 65–72.

Coster, J., & Schwebel, M. (1997). Well-functioning in professional psychologists. *Professional Psychology: Research and Practice, 28,* 5–13.

Covey, S. (1989). *The 7 habits of highly effective people.* New York: Simon & Schuster.

Csikszentmihalyi, M. (1990). *Flow: The psychology of optimal experience.* New York: HarperCollins.

Deci, E. (1975). *Intrinsic motivation.* New York: Plenum.

DeLongis, A., Coyne, J., Dakof, G., Folkman, S., & Lazarus, R. (1982). Relationship of daily hassles, uplifts and major life events to health status. *Health Psychology, 1,* 119–136.

Deutsch, C. (1985). A survey of therapists' personal problems and treatment. *Professional Psychology: Research and Practice, 16,* 305–315.

De Vaney Olvey, C., Hogg, A., & Counts, W. (2002). Licensure requirements: Have we raised the bar too far? *Professional Psychology: Research and Practice, 33,* 323–329.

Dlugos, R., & Friedlander, M. (2001). Passionately committed psychotherapists: A qualitative study of their experiences. *Professional Psychology: Research and Practice, 32,* 298–304.

Dominguez, J., & Robin, V. (1999). *Your money or your life.* New York: Penguin.

Eagle, M. (2001). Reflections of a psychoanalytic therapist. In M. Goldfried (Ed.), *How therapists change.* Washington, DC: American Psychological Association.

Edelwich, J., & Brodsky, A. (1980). *Burn-out: Stages of disillusionment in the helping profession.* New York: Human Services Press.

Edgar, K. (1978). The epiphany of the self via poetry therapy. In A. Lerner (Ed.), *Poetry in the therapeutic experience.* Elmsford, NY: Pergamon.

Epstein, R. (1997, July/August). Why shrinks have so many problems. *Psychology Today,* 58–78.

Faelten, S. (1996). *Food and you.* Emmaus, PA: Rodale Press.

Fanning, P., & Mitchener, H. (2001). *The 50 best ways to simplify your life.* Oakland, CA: New Harbinger.

Farber, B. (1983). The effects of psychotherapeutic practice upon psychotherapists. *Psychotherapy: Theory, Research and Practice, 20,* 174–182.

Farber, B. (1990). Burnout in psychotherapists: Incidence, types and trends. *Psychotherapy in Private Practice, 8,* 35–44.

Figley, C. (1995, September). As quoted in R. Edwards. "Compassion fatigue": When listening hurts. *Monitor on Psychology,* 34.

Figley, C. (Ed.). (2002). *Treating compassion fatigue.* New York: Brunner-Routledge.

Fowler, R. (2000). A lesson in taking our own advice. *Monitor on Psychology, 31*(2), 9.

Fox, R. (1995). The rape of psychotherapy. *Professional Psychology: Research and Practice, 26,* 147–155.

Francis, M., & Pennebaker, J. (1992). Putting stress into words: The impact of writing on physiological, absentee, and self-reported emotional well-being measures. *American Journal of Health Promotion, 6,* 280–286.

Frankl, V. (1959). *Man's search for meaning.* New York: Washington Square Press.

Freudenberger, H. (1986). The healthy professional in treatment: Symptoms, dynamics, and treatment issues. In C. Scott & J. Hawk (Eds.), *Heal thyself: The health of health care professionals.* New York: Brunner-Mazel.

Freudenberger, H., & North, G. (1985). *Women's burnout.* Garden City, NY: Doubleday.

Gabbard, G., & Lester, E. (1995). *Boundaries and boundary violations in psychoanalysis.* New York: Basic Books.

Garling, T., & Evans, G. (Eds.) (1991). *Environment, cognition and action.* London: Oxford University Press.

Gentile, S., Asamen, J., Harmell, P., & Weathers, R. (2002). The stalking of psychologists by their clients. *Professional Psychology: Research and Practice, 33,* 490–494.

Geurts, S., Schaufeli, W., & De Jonge, J. (1998). Burnout and intention to leave among mental health-care professionals. *Journal of Social and Clinical Psychology, 17,* 341–362.

Gibran, K. (1978). *The prophet.* New York: Knopf.

Gilroy, P., Carroll, L., & Murra, J. (2001). Does depression affect clinical practice? A survey of women psychotherapists. *Women and Therapy, 23,* 13–30.

Gilroy, P., Carroll, L., & Murra, J. (2002). A preliminary survey of counseling psychologists' personal experiences with depression and treatment. *Professional Psychology: Research and Practice, 33,* 402– 407.

Golden, V., & Farber, B. (1998). Therapists as parents: Is it good for the children? *Professional Psychology: Research and Practice, 29,* 135–139.

Goldfried, M. (Ed.). (2001). *How therapists change.* Washington, DC: American Psychological Association.

Greenspan, B. (1999, spring). A garden of opportunities: Personal writing for therapists. *The Perspective: A Professional Journal of the Renfrew Foundation, 5,* 4–6.

Grosch, W., & Olsen, D. (1994). *When helping starts to hurt.* New York: Norton.

Groth-Marnat, G., & Edkins, G. (1996). Professional psychologists in general health care settings: A review of the financial efficacy of direct treatment interventions. *Professional Psychology: Research and Practice, 27,* 161–174.

Gruenberg, P. (2001). Boundary violations. In *Ethics premier of the American Psychiatric Association.* Washington, DC: American Psychiatric Association.

Guy, J. (1987). *The personal life of the psychotherapist.* New York: Wiley.

Guy, J. (2000). Self-care corner: Holding the holding environment together: Self-psychology and psychotherapist care. *Professional Psychology: Research and Practice, 31,* 351–352.

Guy, J., Brown, K., & Poelstra, P. (1990). Who gets attacked? A national survey of patient violence directed at psychologists in clinical practice. *Professional Psychology: Research and Practice, 21,* 493–495.

Guy, J., Brown, K., & Poelstra, P. (1992). Safety concerns and protective measures used by psychotherapists. *Professional Psychology: Research and Practice, 23,* 421–423.

Guy, J., Freudenberger, H., Farber, B., & Norcross, J. (1990). Hazards of the psychotherapeutic profession. *Psychotherapy in Private Practice, 8,* 27–61.

Guy, J., Poelstra, P., & Stark, M. (1989). Personal distress and psychotherapeutic effectiveness: National survey of psychologists practicing psychotherapy. *Professional Psychology: Research and Practice, 20,* 48–50.

Haber, S., Rodino, E., & Lipner, I. (2001). *Saying goodbye to managed care: Building your independent psychology practice.* New York: Springer.

Heerwagen, J. (2000). Green buildings, organizational success and occupant productivity. *Building Research and Information, 28,* 353–367.

Herron, W., & Welt, S. (1992). *Money matters: The role of the fee in psychology and psychoanalysis.* New York: Guilford.

Hill, C., & Knox, S. (2001). Self-disclosure. *Psychotherapy: Theory, Research, Practice, Training, 38,* 413–417.

Hill, P., & Pargament, K. (2003). Advances in the conceptualization and measurement of religion and spirituality: Implications for physical and mental health research. *American Psychologist, 58,* 64–74.

Holmes, T., & Masuda, M. (1974). Life change and illness susceptibility. In B. S. Dohrenwend & B. P. Dohrenwend (Eds.), *Stressful life events: Their nature and effects.* New York: Wiley.

Holzman, L., Searight, H. R., & Hughes, H. (1996). Clinical psychology graduate students and personal psychotherapy: Results of an exploratory survey. *Professional Psychology: Research and Practice, 27,* 98–101.

Jackson, H., & Nuttall, R. (2001). A relationship between childhood sexual abuse and professional sexual misconduct. *Professional Psychology: Research and Practice, 32,* 200–204.

Jacobs, L. (2001). Pathways to a relational worldview. In M. Goldfried (Ed.), *How therapists change.* Washington DC: American Psychological Association.

Johnson, W., & Huwe, J. (2003). *Getting mentored in graduate school.* Washington, DC: American Psychological Association.

Kanner, A., Coyne, J., Schaefer, C., & Lazarus, R. (1981). Comparison of two modes of stress management: Daily hassles and uplifts versus major life events. *Journal of Behavioral Medicine, 4,* 1–39.

Kaplan, R., & Kaplan, S. (1989). *The experience of nature.* New York: Cambridge University Press.

Kasser, T. (2002). *The high price of materialism.* Cambridge, MA: MIT Press.

Kearney, D. (1990). Psychologists, well-being and practice. *Educational and Child Psychology, 7,* 15–22.

Klein, A. (1998). *The courage to laugh.* New York: Jeremy P. Tarcher.

Koocher, G., & Keith-Spiegel, P. (1998). *Ethics in psychology: Professional standards and cases.* London: Oxford University Press.

Kottler, J. (1992). *Compassionate therapy: Working with difficult clients.* San Francisco: Jossey-Bass.

Kottler, J. (1993). *On being a therapist.* San Francisco: Jossey-Bass.

Kottler, J., & Hazler, R. (1997). *What you never learned in graduate school: A survival guide for therapists.* New York: Norton.

Kovaks, A. (1997, October). As quoted in T. DeAngelis, Tips for surviving—and thriving—in today's practice. *Monitor on Psychology,* 17.

Kramen-Kahn, B., & Hansen, N. (1998). Rafting the rapids: Occupational hazards, rewards, and coping strategies of psychotherapists. *Professional Psychology: Research and Practice, 29,* 130–134.

Kraut, R., Kiesler, S., Boneva, B., Cummings, J., Helgeson, V., & Crawford, M. (2002). Internet paradox revisisted. *Journal of Social Issues, 58,* 49–74.

Kremer, T., & Gesten, E. (2003). Managed mental health care: The client's perspective. *Professional Psychology: Research and Practice, 34,* 187– 196.

Kuo, F., & Sullivan, W. (2001). Environment and crime in the inner city. Does vegetation reduce crime? *Environment and Behavior, 33,* 343–367.

Lakein, A. (1973). *How to get control of your time and your life.* New York: Signet.

Lamb, D., Catanzaro, S., & Moorman, A. (2003). Psychologists reflect on their sexual relationships with clients, supervisees, and students: Occurrence, impact, rationales, and collegial intervention. *Professional Psychology: Research and Practice, 34,* 102–107.

Lazarus, A. (2000). Multimodal replenishment. *Professional Psychology: Research and Practice, 31,* 93–94.

Lehman, A., & Salovey, P. (1990). Psychotherapist orientation and expectations for liked and disliked patients. *Professional Psychology: Research and Practice, 21,* 385–391.

Leiper, R., & Casares, P. (2000). An investigation of the attachment organization of clinical psychologists and its relationship to clinical practice. *British Journal of Medical Psychology, 73,* 449–464.

Leith, L. (1998). *Exercise your way to better mental health.* Morgantown, WV: Fitness Information Technology.

Le Lieuvre, R. (1998). "Goodnight Saigon": Music, fiction, poetry and film in readjustment group counseling. *Professional Psychology: Research and Practice, 29,* 74–78.

Lerner, A. (Ed.). (1978). *Poetry in the psychotherapeutic experience.* Elmsford, NY: Pergamon.

Levoy, G. (1997). *Callings: Finding and following an authentic life.* New York: Harmony.

Ligiero, D., & Gelso, C. (2002). Countertransference, attachment, and the working alliance: The therapist's contribution. *Psychotherapy: Theory, Research, Practice, Training, 39,* 3–11.

Lion, J., & Herschler, J. (1998). The stalking of clinicians by their patients. In J. Meloy (Ed.), *The psychology of stalking*. San Diego, CA: Academic Press.

Luepker, E. (2002). *Record keeping in psychotherapy and counseling: Protecting confidentiality and the professional relationship*. New York: Brunner-Routledge.

Lyckhom, L. (1998). Should physicians accept gifts from patients? *Journal of the American Medical Association, 280,* 1944–1946.

Maas, J. (1998). *Power sleep*. New York: HarperCollins.

Mackoff, B. (1986). *Leaving the office behind*. New York: Dell.

Macran, S., Stiles, W., & Smith, J. (1999). Why therapists should consider therapy. *Journal of Counseling Psychology, 46,* 419–431.

Mahoney, M. (1997). Psychotherapists' personal problems and self-care patterns. *Professional Psychology: Research and Practice, 28,* 14–16.

Mahoney, M. (2001). Behaviorism, cognitivism, and constructivism: Reflections on people and patterns in my intellectual development. In M. Goldfried (Ed.), *How therapists change*. Washington, DC: American Psychological Association.

Mahrer, A. (2000). How to use psychotherapy on, for, and by oneself. *Professional Psychology: Research and Practice, 31,* 226–229.

Mallinckrodt, B., & Bennett, J. (1992). Social support and the impact of job loss in dislocated blue-collar workers. *Journal of Counseling Psychology, 39,* 482–489.

Maslach, C. (1976). Burned-out. *Human Behavior, 5,* 16–22.

Maslach, C. (1982). *Burnout: The cost of caring*. Englewood Cliffs, NJ: Prentice-Hall.

Maslach, C. (1986). Stress, burnout and workaholism. In R. Kilburg, P. Nathan & R. Thoreson (Eds.), *Professionals in distress*. Washington, DC: American Psychological Association.

Maslach, C., & Leiter, M. (1997). *The truth about burnout*. San Francisco: Jossey-Bass.

McGraw, P. (1999). *Life strategies*. New York: Hyperion.

Meloy, J., & Gothard, S. (1995). A demographic and clinical comparison of obsessional followers and offenders with mental disorders. *American Journal of Psychiatry, 152,* 258–263.

Miller, I. (1996). Managed care is harmful to outpatient mental health services: A call for accountability. *Professional Psychology: Research and Practice, 27,* 349–363.

Miller, W., & Thoresen, C. (2003). Spirituality, religion and health. *American Psychologist, 58,* 24–35.

Moran, C. (2002). Humor as a moderator of compassion fatigue. In C. Figley (Ed.), *Treating compassion fatigue*. New York: Brunner-Routledge.

Nash, J., Norcross, J., & Prochaska, J. (1984). Satisfactions and stresses of independent practice. *Psychotherapy in Private Practice, 2,* 39–48.

Norcross, J. (2000). Psychotherapist self-care: Practitioner-tested, research-informed strategies. *Professional Psychology: Research and Practice, 31,* 710–713.

Norcross, J., & Guy, J. (1989). Ten therapists: The process of becoming and being. In W. Dryden & L. Spurling (Eds.), *On becoming a psychotherapist.* London: Tavistock-Routledge.

Norcross, J., & Prochaska, J. (1982). A national survey of clinical psychologists: Views on training, career choice and APA. *Clinical Psychologist, 35,* 3–6.

Norcross, J., & Prochaska, J. (1983). Psychotherapists in independent practice: Some findings and issues. *Professional Psychology: Research and Practice, 14,* 869–881.

Novaco, R. (1975). *Anger control: The development and evaluation of an experimental treatment.* Lexington, MA: D. C. Heath.

O'Connor, M. (2001). On the etiology and effective management of professional distress and impairment among psychologists. *Professional Psychology: Research and Practice, 32,* 345–350.

O'Connor, E., Peters, L., Rudolf, C., & Pooyan, A. (1982). Situational constraints and employee affective reactions: A partial field replication. *Group and Organizational Studies, 7,* 418–428.

O'Hanlon, B. (2001, October). *Spirituality and psychotherapy.* Workshop presented in Portland, Oregon.

Otto, R., & Schmidt, W. (1991). Malpractice in verbal psychotherapy: Problems and potential solutions. *Forensic Reports, 4,* 309–339.

Page, C. (2001, December). *Intuition: Awakening to our own inner resources.* Workshop presented in Hilton Head, South Carolina.

Parvin, R., & Anderson, G. (1999). What are we worth? Fee decisions of psychologists in private practice. *Women and Therapy, 22,* 15–25.

Pearlman, L., & Maclan, P. (1995). Vicarious traumatization: An empirical study of the effects of trauma work on trauma therapists. *Professional Psychology: Research and Practice, 26,* 558–565.

Pearlman, L., & Saakvitne, K. (1995). *Trauma and the therapist: Countertransference and vicarious traumatization in therapy with incest survivors.* New York: Norton.

Pennebaker, J. (1993). Putting stress into words: Health, linguistic and therapeutic implications. *Behavior Research and Therapy, 31,* 539– 548.

Pennebaker, J., Colder, M., & Sharp, L. (1990). Accelerating the coping process. *Journal of Personality and Social Psychology, 58,* 528–537.

Perlman, L. (2001). Nonspecific, unintended and serendipitous effects in psychotherapy. *Professional Psychology: Research and Practice, 3,* 283–288.

Peterson, Z. (2002). More than a mirror: The ethics of therapist self-disclosure. *Psychotherapy: Theory, Research, Practice, Training, 39,* 21–31.

Phelps, R., Eisman, E., & Kohout, J. (1998). Psychological practice and managed care results of the CAPP practitioner survey. *Professional Psychology: Research and Practice, 29,* 31–36.

Pipal, J. (1997, March). *Private practice sanity.* Workshop presented in Phoenix, Arizona.

Polster, D. (2001). Gifts. In *Ethics premier of the American Psychiatric Association.* Washington, DC: American Psychiatric Association.

Pope, K. (1990). Therapist–patient sex as sex abuse: Six scientific, professional and practical dilemmas in addressing victimization and rehabilitation. *Professional Psychology: Research and Practice, 21,* 227–239.

Pope, K., & Tabachnick, B. (1993). Therapists' anger, hate, fear, and sexual feelings: National survey of therapist responses, client characteristics, critical events, formal complaints, and training. *Professional Psychology: Research and Practice, 24,* 142–152.

Pope, K., Tabachnik, B., & Keith-Spiegel, P. (1987). Ethics of practice: The beliefs and behaviors of psychologists as therapists. *American Psychologist, 42,* 993–1006.

Pope, K., & Vetter, V. (1992). Ethical dilemmas encountered by members of the American Psychological Association. *American Psychologist, 47,* 397–411.

Powell, L., Shahabi, L., & Thoresen, C. (2003). Religion and spirituality: Linkages to physical health. *American Psychologist, 58,* 36–52.

Prochaska, J., & Norcross, J. (1983). Contemporary psychotherapists: A national survey of characteristics, practices, orientations, and attitudes. *Psychotherapy: Theory, Research, and Practice, 20,* 161–173.

Progoff, I. (1992). *At a journal workshop: The basic text and guide for using the Intensive Journal process.* New York: Dialogue House Library.

Quick, J. C., Quick, J. D., & Hurrell, J. (1997). *Preventive stress management in organizations.* Washington, DC: American Psychological Association.

Quindlen, A. (2000). *A short guide to a happy life.* New York: Random House.

Radeke, J., & Mahoney, M. (2000). Comparing the personal lives of psychotherapists and research psychologists. *Professional Psychology: Research and Practice, 31,* 82–84.

Reamer, F. (2001). *Tangled relationships.* New York: Columbia University Press.

Rippere, V., & Williams, R. (Eds.). (1985). *Wounded healers.* New York: Wiley.

Robbins, J., Beck, P., Mueller, D., & Mizener, D. (1988). Therapists' perceptions of difficult psychiatric patients. *Journal of Nervous and Mental Diseases, 176,* 490–496.

Rodolfa, E., Kraft, W., & Reilley, R. (1988). Stressors of professionals and trainees at APA-approved counseling and V.A. Medical Center internship sites. *Professional Psychology: Research and Practice, 19,* 43–49.

Romans, J., Hays, J., & White, T. (1996). Stalking and related behaviors experienced by counseling center staff members from current or former clients. *Professional Psychology: Research and Practice, 27,* 595–599.

Ronnestad, M., & Skovholt, T. (2001). Learning arenas for professional development: Retrospective accounts of senior psychotherapists. *Professional Psychology: Research and Practice, 32,* 181–187.

Roos, P., & Cohen, L. (1987). Sex roles and social support as moderators of life stress adjustment. *Journal of Personality and Social Psychology, 52,* 576–585.

Samuels, M., & Samuels, N. (1992). *Seeing with the mind's eye: The history, techniques and uses of visualization.* New York: Random House.

Sanchez, L., & Turner, S. (2003). Practicing psychology in the era of managed care. *American Psychologist, 58,* 116–129.

Sawyer, D. (2002, June). Do what you love. *Reader's Digest,* 143–145.

Schauben, L., & Frazier, P. (1995). Vicarious trauma: The effects on female counselors of working with sexual violence survivors. *Psychology of Women Quarterly, 19,* 49–64.

Schwebel, M., Skorina, J., & Schoener, G. (1994). *Assisting impaired psychologists* (revised). Washington, DC: American Psychological Association.

Seeman, T., Dubin, L., & Seeman, M. (2003). Religiosity/spirituality and health: A critical review of the evidence for biological pathways. *American Psychologist, 58,* 53–63.

Seligman, M. (1975). *Helplessness: On depression, development and death.* San Francisco: Freeman.

Seligman, M. (1994). *What you can change and what you can't.* New York: Knopf.

Seligman, M. (1995). The effectiveness of psychotherapy: The *Consumer Reports* study. *American Psychologist, 50,* 965–974.

Seligman, M. (2002). *Authentic happiness: Using the new positive psychology to realize your potential for lasting fulfillment.* New York: Free Press.

Sherman, M. (1996). Distress and professional impairment due to mental health problems among psychologists. *Clinical Psychology Review, 16,* 299–315.

Sherman, M., & Thelen, M. (1998). Distress and professional impairment among psychologists in clinical practice. *Professional Psychology: Research and Practice,* 29, 79–85.

Sinetar, M. (1987). *Do what you love, the money will follow.* New York: Dell.

Skovholt, T., & Ronnestad, M. (1995). *The evolving professional self: Stages and themes in therapist and counselor development.* New York: Wiley.

Skovholt, T., & Ronnestad, M. (2001). The long, textured path from novice to senior practitioner. In T. Skovholt (Ed.), *The resilient practitioner: Burnout prevention and self-care strategies for counselors, therapists, teachers and health professionals.* Needham Heights, MA: Allyn & Bacon.

Soisson, E., VandeCreek, L., & Knapp, S. (1987). Thorough record keeping: A good defense in a litigious era. *Professional Psychology: Research and Practice, 18,* 498–502.

Solomon, G., Heisberger, J., & Winer, J. (1981). Confidentiality issues in rural community mental health. *Journal of Rural Community Psychology, 2,* 17–31.

Spector, P., Dwyer, D., & Jex, S. (1988). Relation of job stressors to affective, health, and performance outcomes: A comparison of multiple data sources. *Journal of Applied Psychology, 73,* 11–19.

Stadler, H. (1990). Counselor impairment. In B. Herlihy & L. Golden (Eds.), *Ethical standards casebook.* Alexandria, VA: American Counseling Association.

Sternberg, R. (2003, July/August). To be civil. *Monitor on Psychology,* 5.

St. James, E. (1994). *Simplify your life.* New York: Hyperion.

Stricker, G. (2001). How I learned to abandon certainty and embrace change. In M. Goldfriend (Ed.), *How therapists change.* Washington DC: American Psychological Association.

Stromberg, C., Schneider, J., & Joondeph, B. (1993). Dealing with potentially dangerous clients. *The Psychologist's Legal Update, 2,* 1–12.

Sussman, M. (Ed.). (1992). *A curious calling: Unconscious motivations for practicing psychotherapy.* Northvale, NJ: Jason Aronson.

Sussman, M. (Ed.). (1995). *A perilous calling: The hazards of psychotherapy practice.* New York: Wiley.

Tett, R., Bobocel, D., Hafer, C., Lees, M., Smith, C., & Jackson, D. (1992). The dimensionality of type A behavior within a stressful work situation. *Journal of Personality, 60,* 533–551.

Tishler, Gordon, L., & Landry-Meyer, L. (2000). Managing the violent patient: A guide for psychologists and other mental health professionals. *Professional Psychology: Research and Practice, 31,* 34–41.

Tubesing, D. (1978, May). *Stress skills.* Workshop presented in Phoenix, Arizona.

Ulrich, R. (1984). View through a window may influence recovery from surgery. *Science, 224,* 420–421.

Ulrich, R. (1991). Effects of healthy facility interior design on wellness: Theory and scientific research. *Journal of Health Care Design, 3,* 97–109.

Warner, R. (2000). *Get a life.* Berkeley, CA: Nolo.

Weinberg, G. (1984). *The heart of psychotherapy.* New York: St. Martin's Press.

Weiss, L. (1992). *Dream analysis in psychotherapy.* Needham Heights, MA: Allyn & Bacon.

Weiss, L. (1999). *Practical dreaming: Awakening the power of dreams in your life.* Oakland, CA: New Harbinger.

Welt, S., & Herron, W. (1990). *Narcissism and the psychotherapist.* New York: Guilford.

Williams, M. (2000). Victimized by "victims": A taxonomy of antecedents of false complaints against psychotherapists. *Professional Psychology: Research and Practice, 31,* 75–81.

Wittenberg, K., & Norcross, J. (2001). Practitioner perfectionism: Relationship to ambiguity tolerance and work satisfaction. *Journal of Clinical Psychology, 57,* 1543–1550.

Wrzesniewski, A., McCauley, C., Rozin, P., & Schwartz, B. (1997). Jobs, careers, and callings: People's relations to their work. *Journal of Research in Personality, 31,* 21–33.

Yalom, I. (2002). *The gift of therapy.* New York: HarperCollins.

Ziegler, J., & Kanas, N. (1986). Coping with stress during internship. In C. Scott & J. Hawk (Eds.), *Heal thyself: The health of health care professionals.* New York: Brunner-Mazel.

Index